TableTalk

A Cookbook
and Memoir

About the Author

Dorothy Firestone refused to major in English because it involved writing. She refused to buy a food processor because "who wants to cook that much." About 30 years ago, she realized that writing and cooking were what she really wanted to do, and she has been doing both ever since. (She is on her third computer and third food processor.) For over twenty years, she wrote free-lance food features for the *St. Louis Post-Dispatch* and for several magazines. For twelve years, she wrote the *TableTalk* column in the *St. Louis Jewish Light*. In *TableTalk: A Cookbook and Memoir*, she has brought together her favorite foods and food stories. She lives in St. Louis, Missouri with her husband, Billy Firestone, and enjoys cooking for her children, grandchildren and friends.

About the Artist

Nearly fifty years ago, Amy Firestone Rosen began her career in fine art with chalk on sidewalk and crayon on shirt board. By1980, she had become a graphic designer, developing logos and brochures and designing posters and books. Five years ago, she returned to fine art, studying printmaking and painting. Her work has been celebrated in many juried shows in the St.Louis area. Rosen lives in St. Louis with her husband Mark Rosen and their daughters Emily and Jessica.

Copyright © 2007 by Dorothy Firestone

Cover art, interior art and layout design by Amy Firestone Rosen

Library of Congress Control Number: 2007905494

ISBN 13: 978-0-615-15498-5

Published by Dorothy P. Firestone, 2007, St. Louis, Missouri

**In memory of Jim Firestone
whose dream refrigerator had no doors.**

**For Ben, Joanna, Emily, Jessica, Adam, Shane and Lily
with love**

Contents

Onion, detail
Waterless Lithography 19" x 19".

Thanks

- To Billy Firestone for supporting my project and tasting everything.
- To Amy Firestone Rosen for art and design.
- To Jim Firestone and to my mother, Sadie Peskind, for their presence throughout the book.
- To Fred Firestone and Mark Rosen for encouragement.
- To Marilyn Firestone and Nancy Kalishman for editing.
- To Marcella and Victor Hazan for sharing Italy.
- To Mark Bittman, Marion Burros, Bill Cardwell, Marcella Hazan and Danny Meyer for permission to reprint recipes.
- To Judith Aronson, Joy Dunkelman, Marilyn Firestone, Elaine Gernstein, Evelyn Goldberg, Nancy Kalishman, Peggy Lents, Carolyn and Joe Losos, Ruth McKinney, Joy Melman, Candy Meyers, Amy Firestone Rosen, Audrey Rothbarth, Renée Samson, Ina Schnell, Mitzi and Dick Sisson and Patty Walsh for recipes and suggestions.

Credits

Most of the stories in *TableTalk: A Cookbook and Memoir* appeared in slightly altered form in the *St. Louis Jewish Light* and in the *St. Louis Post-Dispatch.*

Many of the recipes are those of cookbook writers and chefs whom I interviewed. Four of the recipes were winners in *TableTalk* contests. Some are those of my family and friends, and the rest have come from my kitchen. All the recipes have been tested, tasted and eaten.

Introduction

For over twenty-five years, I wrote stories with recipes for magazines and newspapers and, for twelve years, the *TableTalk* column in the *St. Louis Jewish Light. TableTalk: A Cookbook and Memoir* combines my favorites.

The book, however, did not begin as memoir. It was to be a cookbook for our grandchildren, which indeed it is. Most of the recipes are for beginning cooks, meant to give them the pleasures of the table from their own kitchens.

But as the book began to take shape, and the number of family stories grew, I realized I was writing both cookbook and memoir. Indeed, memories came tumbling out of my pantry.

Food has the power to awaken memories. A whiff of apple pie baking on a cool autumn day takes me back to my mother's kitchen. A taste of Quickles and I am in the summers of my childhood, and with a spoonful of Sunshine Soup, Billy and I are in Kyoto, 1985.

The Onion

Concentric layers cast in papery skin
In yellow, white or red, with shoots of green
If too ripe, rounded, flat, or slightly thin,
An enigmatic root, with powers unseen
That penetrate the nose, the throat, the eye
With fumes so pungent we begin to weep,
Eyes on fire, the only reason why
From onions minced into a tidy heap.
But thinly sliced atop a red tomato
Or bathed in butter in a frying pan,
Curried, braised or souped with a potato
Or grilled or eaten crisp straight from a can,
Boiled, roasted, baked in any measure,
Onions turn our weeping into pleasure.

Dorothy Firestone

Appetizers

Bounce, *detail*
India ink wash on canvas. 4' x 4'

A Day in Jerusalem

On a cool Friday afternoon on our first day in Jerusalem, Billy and I wandered through the streets of the Mea Sharim, that part of the city inhabited by ultra Orthodox Jews.

"You looking for someone?" a man who sounded like an American asked. "No," we said. "We are just looking around." "Have you ever been in an Israeli home?" he asked. "No? Well, come with me."

David, our host, told us that he and his wife Leah had moved from Pittsburgh to Jerusalem a few years ago, looking for a more religious community. He took Billy with him into a front room while I stayed behind in the kitchen where Leah was blistering an eggplant over a gas flame. The kitchen was warm, filled with the aromas of cooking.

"You Jewish?" she asked. "Yes, of course," I said. "You go to the mikva? You observe the Sabbath?" I said "no" to the mikva and waffled on the Sabbath.

She showed me the pot of cholent she was preparing for Sabbath lunch. Cholent, known as Sabbath stew, is a stew made of meat or beans and vegetables that cooks unattended in a slow oven all night for Sabbath lunch the next day.

She offered me some gefilte fish she had just prepared. It was the first time I had ever tasted hot gefilte fish–ours comes cold out of a jar. It was firm and well seasoned.

Meanwhile, in the living room, filled with small shiva stools, David introduced Billy to a friend who had come to call. "I am in mourning for my mother," David said. "Will you join us in prayers? "I would be happy to," Billy said, "but I can't read Hebrew. I was never a Bar Mitzvah."

"Never a Bar Mitzvah?" the men said in unison. "We'll make you one right now."

They strapped tefillin on him, handed him a yarmulke and tallis, and told him to repeat the prayers after them. "Congratulations," they said at the conclusion of the ten-minute service. "You are now a Bar Mitzvah." Just then, I walked into the room with some gefilte fish for Billy to taste.

"I just became a Bar Mitzvah," he said.

"But you didn't invite me," I said.

We knew the Bar Mitzvah was not an official Bar Mitzvah, but that afternoon was one of the high points of our trip to Israel because David and Leah showed us a part of Jerusalem not in our tour books.

And to commemorate the occasion, even though I had not been invited, I bought Billy a leather cigar case.

Roasted Eggplant Caponata

Makes 1½-2 cups

Even eggplant-haters like this Caponata.

1 eggplant, about 1¼ pounds
¼ cup walnuts
¼ cup minced sweet onion
¼ cup minced fresh parsley
1 small jalapeño pepper, seeded and minced
1 garlic clove, peeled and minced
½ teaspoon kosher salt
Freshly ground black pepper, to taste
1 tablespoon fresh lemon juice or to taste
2 tablespoons extra virgin olive oil

1. Prick the eggplant all over with a fork. Microwave it at full power uncovered until it is soft and collapsed, about 10 minutes. Set aside to cool.

2. Microwave the walnuts until fragrant and toasted, about 2½ to 3 minutes. When cool, chop them.

3. Scrape the meat from the eggplant skin and chop it coarsely. Discard the skin.

4. Combine the eggplant with the walnuts, onion, parsley, jalapeño, garlic, salt, pepper and lemon juice in a large bowl. Slowly, whisk in the olive oil. Taste to check the seasoning. Cover and refrigerate until 1 hour before serving.

Note:
Jalepeño can be quite hot. Start with a bit and add as needed.

Almost Homemade Gefilte Fish

Serves 4-6

This was Mother's way to enhance purchased gefilte fish.

1 quart purchased gefilte fish •
½ cup water
1 carrot, peeled and sliced thin
1 medium onion, peeled and sliced thin
1 tablespoon sugar
½ teaspoon white pepper
1 teaspoon kosher salt
Parsley to garnish

1. Drain the broth from the fish. Set the fish aside. Combine the broth, water, carrot, onion, sugar, white pepper and salt in a skillet large enough to hold the fish in 1 layer. Simmer uncovered about 10 minutes, until vegetables are tender.

2. Add the fish and simmer uncovered 3 minutes more. Refrigerate the fish in the liquid. When cool, cover it.

3. Garnish with the carrot slices and parsley. Serve with horseradish.

• If possible, avoid buying fish with monosodium glutamate, an unnecessary seasoning added by many manufacturers.

Note:
If you wish a "seconds" platter, arrange the fish in a shallow bowl; garnish each piece with carrot and parsley and a few spoonfuls of the broth. Cover with plastic wrap. The broth will jell, holding everything in place.

Halved Avocados with Balsamic Vinaigrette

Makes about 1⅓ cups vinaigrette

This is a stunning but simple first course.

⅓ cup balsamic vinegar
2 tablespoons minced fresh basil or 2 teaspoons dried
2-3 minced garlic cloves
Kosher salt and freshly ground pepper to taste
1 cup extra virgin olive oil
3 ripe avocados
1 lime cut into 6 wedges

1. Combine the vinegar, basil, garlic, salt and pepper in a blender, food processor or jar with a lid. Blend until well mixed.

2. Add the oil in a slow, steady stream and blend well. Taste and adjust seasoning. Refrigerate up to 1 week. Shake well before using.

3. Just before serving, cut the avocados in half, remove the pits and fill the cavities with the vinaigrette. Serve with lime wedges.

Note:
Ripe avocados yield to gentle palm pressure.

Guacamole

Makes about 1 cup

The guacamole is best prepared right before serving.

3 tablespoons chopped fresh cilantro, divided
1½ tablespoons chopped white onion
½ small jalapeño, seeded and chopped
1 teaspoon kosher salt
2 large ripe avocados
1 large tomato, seeded, juiced and diced, reserving 1 tablespoon for garnish
Juice of ½ lime
Blue corn chips

1. Mash 2 tablespoons of the cilantro, the onion, jalapeño and salt into a paste with a mortar and pestle, spoon or potato masher.

2. Cut the avocados in halves; remove the pits and reserve them. Scoop the flesh into the paste and mash, coarsely. Add the tomato and lime juice. Taste to adjust the seasoning.

3. Transfer to a serving dish and top with the avocado pits to keep the guacamole from darkening. Cover with plastic wrap pressing against the surface. Refrigerate until serving time.

4. Remove the pits but save them to top any left over guacamole. Garnish with remaining cilantro and tomato and serve with blue corn chips.

Note:
Ripe avocados yield to gentle palm pressure.

Crostini with Tomatoes and Basil

Serves 8

These are the ultimate toasted cheese sandwiches, good with cocktails, soups or salads.

1½ cups chopped or coarsely grated cheese such as Asiago, Parmesan, Mozzarella or a combination
½ cup coarsely chopped fresh basil or 2 tablespoons dry crumbled basil if it is aromatic
1 cup diced fresh tomatoes, with skin, juices and seeds
3 to 5 small garlic cloves, peeled and minced
½ cup coarsely chopped black kalamata olives or ripe black olives
24 (¼-inch thick) slices of dense French or Italian baguette

1. Combine the cheese, basil, tomatoes, garlic and olives several hours or the day before serving Crostini. Taste to adjust seasoning.

2. Several hours before serving, spread the mixture on bread slices and place them on a baking pan; cover with waxed paper.

3. Preheat the oven to 350 degrees. Remove the waxed paper. Bake the Crostini about 5 to 8 minutes or until melted and bubbly. Serve immediately.

Note:
Allow 3 Crostini per person and bake only as needed so they are served hot.

Deviled Eggs

4 servings

Deviled Eggs have been popular as long as there have been picnics.

4 eggs
½ teaspoon Dijon mustard
4 teaspoons sweet pickle relish
1 teaspoon minced sweet onion
2 tablespoons mayonnaise
Kosher salt and freshly ground pepper to taste
Optional: capers, hot pepper flakes, anchovies
Paprika and minced fresh parsley to garnish

1. To hard boil the eggs, put them into a saucepan and cover them with water by one inch. Do not cover the pan. Bring to a boil, take the pan off the heat, cover it and let the eggs sit 11 minutes. Put the eggs into iced water until they are cool. (Chilling makes them easier to peel.)

2. Peel the eggs and cut them in half lengthwise. Put the yolks in a bowl; set the whites aside.

3. Mash the yolks with a fork and combine with the mustard, relish, onion, mayonnaise, salt and pepper to taste. Add whatever else you like. Taste to check the seasoning. Divide among the egg whites. Smooth the tops and garnish with sprinkles of paprika and parsley. Refrigerate until serving.

Hummus

Makes about 2 cups

The red bell pepper adds color and flavor to the hummus.

1 (15-ounce) can chickpeas
¼ cup tahini
2 teaspoons minced garlic
3 tablespoons fresh lemon juice
1½ teaspoons ground cumin
1 teaspoon kosher salt
1 tablespoon water
1 red bell pepper, seeded and diced
Freshly ground black pepper to taste

1. Rinse and drain the chickpeas.

2. Put everything in a food processor and process until finely mixed and smooth. Taste to check the seasoning. Stuff celery or endive with it, or serve it with pita bread or blue corn chips.

Lentil Pâté

Makes about 2 cups

It's not chopped liver, but it fools a lot of people.

1½ cups chopped onion, divided
1½ tablespoons extra virgin olive oil
½ cup lentils
½ cup chopped walnuts
1 hard-boiled egg
1 teaspoon kosher salt or to taste
Freshly ground pepper

1. Put 1¼ cups chopped onion and the oil in a heavy saucepan, cover and cook slowly until the onion starts to brown, about 30 minutes. Set aside.

2. Rinse the lentils and put them in another saucepan with 2 cups water. Simmer partly covered about 40 minutes or until tender. Scoop out ½ cup cooking water and set aside. Drain the lentils and set aside.

3. Toast walnuts in the microwave uncovered for 2½ minutes. Set aside.

4. Put the sautéed onion, lentils, walnuts, egg, remaining onion and salt and pepper in a food processor. Process until smooth.

5. If the pâté seems dry, add a tablespoon of the reserved lentil cooking water. Taste to check the seasoning. Cover the pâté and refrigerate.

6. Remove from the refrigerator 1 hour before serving. Serve with crackers as an appetizer or with dark bread and lettuce for a sandwich. Keeps refrigerated up to 3 days.

Sugar Roasted Nuts

Good with cocktails or tossed in salads

1 egg white
1 tablespoon water
¾ pound pecans or walnuts
½ cup sugar
½ teaspoon kosher salt
½ teaspoon cinnamon
¼ teaspoon cayenne pepper

1. Preheat the oven to 225 degrees.

2. Beat the egg white with water; stir in the nuts.

3. Combine the sugar, salt, cinnamon and pepper in a bag.

4. Shake the nuts in the bag. Spread them on a large pan with sides and bake 1 hour, stirring every 15 minutes. When cool, refrigerate them.

A Short History of That Little Something

For a nation of English speaking people, we toss out French terms as though we knew the language. We call that little something served before a meal an hors d'oeuvre. The French term hors d'oeuvre translates literally as "outside the work," which came to mean "dishes outside the meal." Hors d'oeuvres can be fancy canapés or simple selections of crudités.

Canapé? Crudités? Canapé is French for couch or settee, but in culinary matters, a canapé is a small decorative piece of bread, toasted or not, topped with something savory such as anchovy, cheese or some type of spread. Crudités are raw seasonal vegetables frequently served with a dipping sauce.

The Romans were the first to serve small portions of foods at the beginning of a meal meant to stimulate the appetite and aid in digestion. The Italians followed with antipasti; the Greeks, meze; the Spanish, tapas; and Ashkenazic Jews, forespice.

Whatever you choose to call them, appetizers should be taken in moderation so they do not detract from the main course. On the other hand, many appetizers make good lunches, light suppers or side dishes.

Crudités

Serves 10-12

Some prefer crudités alone; others like them with a dip or sauce. They go especially well with Liptauer Cheese. Select from the list of ingredients to total 3 quarts of vegetables.

One head kale
1 tablespoon kosher salt
3 cups cauliflower bite-size florets
3 cups broccoli bite-size florets
1 pound fresh green beans, trimmed and left whole
½ pound carrots, peeled and sliced into 3-inch sticks
2 medium cucumbers, peeled only if the skin is tough or waxed, sliced into spears
3 celery ribs, peeled and sliced into 3-inch sticks
1 bunch red radishes, trimmed and left whole
1 bunch white radishes, peeled and left whole
1 pound baby turnips, trimmed and left whole
3 bell peppers in various colors, sliced into strips
1 pint cocktail or grape tomatoes
1 (6-ounce) can pitted black olives

1. Separate the kale into leaves. Wash them in cold water, dry on terrycloth towels, wrap well and set them aside in the refrigerator.

2. Have a bowl of ice water ready. Bring a large pot of water to a boil. Stir in the salt, and when the water returns to a boil, drop in the cauliflower. Boil about 2 minutes. Remove the cauliflower with a slotted spoon and chill it in the ice water. Do the same with the broccoli and the green beans. Drain the vegetables and dry them on terrycloth towels. Blanching them in this manner preserves their colors. Wrap the chilled vegetables and refrigerate them.

3. Prepare the carrots, cucumbers, celery, radishes, turnips and peppers. Refrigerate them in plastic bags.

4. To serve, line a basket or tray with the kale leaves. Arrange the crudités on the leaves and garnish them with the tomatoes and olives.

Roasted Red Peppers

Serves 6

These red peppers are good as appetizers or salads.

3 red bell peppers
3 tomatoes
2 garlic cloves
12 anchovies
2 tablespoons extra virgin olive oil
Freshly ground pepper

1. Preheat the oven to 350 degrees. Cut the peppers in halves, discarding stem, seeds and ribs. Rinse and set them aside to drain.

2. Core and dice the tomatoes. Mince the garlic. Dice the anchovies.

3. Divide the tomatoes, garlic and anchovies among the pepper halves. Drizzle with the olive oil. Sprinkle with pepper.

4. Place the peppers in a shallow baking dish and bake 50 to 60 minutes. Serve cold on lettuce-lined plates.

Roasted Garlic

Roasted garlic is wonderful spread on good bread or puréed and mixed into mashed potatoes.

Preheat the oven to 375 degrees.

1. To roast garlic cloves, peel them, • toss with extra virgin olive oil and place them in a single layer on aluminum foil. Fold the foil to enclose the cloves, place on a baking pan and bake until the garlic is slightly browned and fragrant, about 30 minutes. Cool. Place in an airtight container and refrigerate. To serve, purée and blend with butter for roasted garlic toast or mix into mashed potatoes. Or serve roasted cloves whole to spread on bread or crackers.

2. To roast whole garlic bulbs, remove extra parchment-like membrane from the bulbs. With a sharp knife, slice off about ¼-inch from the top of bulbs. Coat with extra virgin olive oil and bake as above. Cool. Place in an airtight container and refrigerate. Serve each person a whole bulb to squeeze onto bread or crackers.

• There is a fine tool to peel garlic. It is a tube about an inch in diameter. You put a clove in the tube and roll the tube on the counter top. The garlic emerges peeled and smooth.

Liptauer Cheese

Makes about 1 cup

This version of the famous Liptauer Cheese, named for a province in Hungary, is also wonderful for lunch the next day.

8 ounces softened cream cheese or Neufchatel
2 scallions, chopped
1 (2-ounce) can or jar of flat anchovy fillets, drained
1 teaspoon paprika
½ teaspoon caraway seeds
1 teaspoon capers, drained

1. Combine the cream cheese with the scallions, anchovies, paprika and caraway seed in a food processor. Process about 1 minute or until the cheese is well mixed.

2. Stir in the capers. Serve with dark bread, crackers or crudités.

Hot Artichoke Spread

Makes about 2 cups

It's good hot and good when it cools down.

1 cup mayonnaise
1⅛ cups freshly grated Parmesan cheese, divided
1 (13¾-ounces) can artichoke hearts, well drained and chopped either by hand or
    briefly in a food processor
¼ teaspoon Worcestershire Sauce or to taste
¼ teaspoon Tabasco Sauce or to taste
Paprika

1. Preheat the oven to 350 degrees. Combine the mayonnaise with 1 cup
    Parmesan in a 2-cup soufflé or baking dish.

2. Stir in the artichokes, Worcestershire and Tabasco. Sprinkle with the remaining
    Parmesan and paprika.

3. Bake about 35 minutes until bubbly. Let the spread cool a few minutes before
    serving with crackers or bread.

Soups

Firefly, *detail*
India Ink wash on canvas. 4' x 4'.

In Search of Lacquer Ware Bowls

In November, 1985, while on an Opera Theatre of St. Louis tour to the Far East, Billy and I gave up a trip to a shrine in Kyoto in order to search for red and black lacquer ware bowls like those our soup was served in the night before. On the first floor of Takashimaya, Kyoto's premier department store, we saw the bowls we wanted, lacquered in red and black, with matching domed lids. While we struggled to translate the yen into dollars, a small Japanese woman approached us.

"I'm bilingual," she said, "I don't work for the store—I'm a customer also—but it sounds as though you need a little help with the yen."

We showed her the bowls we were admiring. "Ah," she said. "They are antique— four hundred dollars for five bowls, a once-in-a-lifetime experience. Let's go to the seventh floor where things are on sale."

We introduced ourselves on the escalator en route to the sale tables where we found bowls—in our price range—lacquered in black on the inside, red on the outside and banded with gold plum blossoms that Toshiko Hasegawa said bring good luck. We were so pleased with meeting our new friend, we invited her to lunch at the Miyako Hotel. "Too expensive," she said. "That would be a once-in-a-life time experience."

When we suggested she choose the place, she said to me after some thought, "Can your husband afford twelve dollars each?" I said he could, and off we went through the streets and alleys of Kyoto to the restaurant.

Although we ate at western tables and chairs, the food and service were decidedly Japanese. The waitress, garbed in kimono, brought us each a lacquered tray—a bento box–fitted with small bowls containing sashimi (sliced fresh raw fish), wasabi (Japanese horseradish), tempura (lightly breaded and fried fish and vegetables), sushi (rice flavored with sweetened rice vinegar and wrapped in seaweed), pickles, rice and soup.

Toshiko told us to sip our soup first and to eat the rice and pickles last. We ate with chopsticks, down to the last grain of soft sticky rice. Over cups of hot green tea, she told us why she spoke English so well.

"It is not a happy story, something I do not talk about often," she said, "but I will tell it to you. But let me say, I am still surprised that I stopped to talk to you. I never do that."

Her parents moved to San Francisco when she was an infant, and when she was fifteen, they sent her to Tokyo to live with a foster family in order to learn Japanese ways and traditions. "And then came Pearl Harbor," she said. "My parents were interned in a concentration camp in California. One of my brothers fought with the Japanese army, the other with the American. They never reconciled, and I have not been back to the United States since." She paused and then said, "Would you like to have coffee in my home?"

Well-kept gardens surrounded her home near an old shrine. (It was the shrine featured in Yasunari Kawabata's *Thousand Cranes* I had read on the plane to Japan.) After changing our shoes for slippers set by the door, we toured the home she shared with her journalist husband. All the floors were covered with rush mats. There were three rooms on the first floor along with a modern kitchen and a bathroom with the meter-deep Japanese-style tub. Upstairs were three rooms. On the floor of one of them were futons equipped with reading lights and electric blankets. Few Japanese homes have central heating, she told us, and so electric blankets, space heaters and heaters mounted under tables take away the chill.

While we drank excellent coffee from her electric coffee maker, she showed us her electric rice cooker, which keeps rice hot and fresh tasting for hours. Her refrigerator had three exterior doors: one to the freezer, one to the main part of the refrigerator and one to the fruit and vegetable keeper. She pulled out pumpkin and green peppers, pre-sliced and packaged at the market, and apples. From the freezer, she took fish purchased marinated in miso paste, a condiment of fermented soybean and salt. There were frozen boned chicken legs and thighs, which Japanese prefer to breasts, she said, and beef, sliced paper-thin.

She planned to have fish along with pumpkin, peppers and apples for dinner. "They are in season now," she said. "Japanese eat fruits and vegetables only when they are in their season."

We commented that the Japanese diet seemed to be a healthy one, with lots of fish, fruits and vegetables and little red meat.

"But there is too much salt in our diet, with miso paste and soy sauce," she said, "even though there is very little fat. And now, many Japanese love the hamburgers and French fries at McDonald's. We do not yet know what effect these foods will have on the traditional Japanese diet."

After an hour's visit, she called a taxi to take us back to our hotel. We put on our shoes and said good-bye. Toshiko stood at the gate to her garden, waving and bowing until the taxi had turned the corner.

When we arrived home, we wrote Toshiko to thank her for her hospitality. She wrote back: "I am happy to know you left Japan with good impressions and also that it was not a tourist superficial view. We have numerous visitors each year in Kyoto, but what they see is an arranged trip of temples and shrines and not a glimpse of how the people, ordinary citizens, live.

"I am glad that I summoned up the courage to talk to you, total strangers. I thank you for trusting me and coming to my home."

Sunshine Soup

Makes about 8 cups

A soup like this one sent us in search of lacquer ware bowls. It's perfect for a cold grey winter day served in lacquer ware bowls with plum blossoms.

2 tablespoons extra virgin olive oil
¼ cup minced shallots
1 butternut squash, about 1¼ pounds, peeled and cubed •
1 sweet potato, about 1 pound, peeled and cubed
6 cups chicken stock, homemade or canned
1 tablespoon minced fresh ginger
Kosher salt and white pepper to taste
1 teaspoon dried ginger if flavors need heightening, optional

1. Warm the oil in a heavy pan; add the shallots and sauté on medium heat about 4 minutes or until golden.

2. Add the squash, sweet potato, stock and fresh ginger. Simmer partly covered for 20 minutes or until the squash and potatoes are tender. Purée.

3. Season to taste with salt and pepper and dried ginger. Refrigerate or freeze the soup if not serving immediately. To serve, garnish with clippings of fresh green herbs.

• Cut the squash into halves and then into fourths. Discard the seeds. Use a vegetable peeler to peel each section down to the orange flesh.

Bean and Barley Soup

Makes about 8 cups

Billy and I ate this smooth bean soup with its bite of barley in Friuli-Venezia, north of Venice.

1½ cups dry pinto or great northern beans
3 tablespoons extra virgin olive oil
2 celery ribs, sliced
2 medium carrots, sliced
1 medium onion, sliced
1 leek or another onion, sliced
1 garlic clove, minced
½ teaspoon dried thyme or 1 teaspoon fresh
1 bay leaf
6 cups chicken stock, homemade or canned
⅔ cup Italian tomatoes, diced, with juice
3 teaspoons kosher salt, divided
6 tablespoons barley
Minced fresh herbs to garnish

1. Soak the beans overnight in water to cover. The next day, drain, rinse and drain them again. Set aside.

2. Warm the oil in a second large pot over medium-high heat. Add the celery, carrot, onion, leek, garlic, thyme and bay leaf and sauté about 8 minutes, until the vegetables are fairly limp but not browned.

3. Stir in the drained beans. Add stock, tomatoes and 2 teaspoons salt. Simmer covered 45 to 50 minutes, until the beans are tender. Remove the bay leaf. Purée the entire soup or purée one cup of the solids to thicken it.

4. Add the barley to 1 quart of water with remaining salt. Simmer covered about 40 minutes until tender but firm. Drain, reserving the liquid.

5. Add the cooked barley to the soup and cook 10 minutes more. If the soup is too thick, thin it with tablespoons of barley cooking water.

6. Garnish soup with minced fresh herbs.

Danny Meyer: Pride of St. Louis

Danny Meyer could well be called the Pride of St. Louis, rivaling any sports figure. He commands the cream of New York restaurants: Union Square Café, Gramercy Tavern, Eleven Madison Park, Tabla, Blue Smoke and Jazz, Shake Shack, The Modern, Cafe 2, Terrace 5 and Hudson Yards Catering.

I interviewed Meyer by phone shortly after September 11th, 2001, before his visit to St. Louis where he was to speak at the Jewish Book Festival about *Second Helpings from Union Square Café* (HarperCollins, 2001), the cookbook that he wrote with Michael Romano. When I asked him what effect he thought the terrorists' attacks would have on home cooking, he said that no one knew what the ripple effect would be.

But when I spoke with him in 2003, he was optimistic. "Home cooking is alive and doing well," he said. "I think there are a lot of people who put in wine cellars and redid kitchens in the roaring 1990's. Now, they are enjoying their homes, dining at home more and having people over more."

Furthermore, he said that home cooks are becoming more adventurous. They are influenced by restaurants, which in turn are influenced by the fresh seasonal foods readily available in Farmers' Markets. "The whole thing is symbiotic," he said. "There is a positive correlation between a restaurant's interest in using seasonal ingredients and the simplicity of its cooking, the kind of cooking you can reproduce at home."

Meyer has interests in food that extend well beyond his restaurants. He is involved with Share Our Strength, a national hunger relief organization, and City Harvest, a perishable food provider that sends foods from restaurants to where they are needed. And he has published another book: *Setting the Table—The Transforming Power of Hospitality in Business* (HarperCollins, 2006).

Meyer said he is often asked why the young people who greet you at his restaurants look and sound like Midwesterners. He said that at first, they were Midwesterners, because he would not hire anyone from New York. "You had to be from west of the Mississippi," he said. "What I did was probably against the law. But I soon learned that the Midwest had no monopoly on the attributes I wanted in my employees.

"There is a group of emotional skills that we try to identify," he said. "I learned this back in St. Louis.

Butternut Squash and Bean Soup

Adapted from *Second Helpings from Union Square Cafe* by Danny Meyer and Michael Romano (HarperCollins, 2001)

Makes about 12 servings

This vegetarian soup is filling and satisfying. Add a salad and you've got supper.

1 pound dried cannellini or navy beans
2 bay leaves
2 tablespoons kosher salt, divided
6 tablespoons extra virgin olive oil
1 large onion, diced
1 large carrot, sliced
2 celery ribs, sliced
1 medium parsnip, diced
1 garlic clove, minced
8-10 large fresh sage leaves tied in a bundle with kitchen twine
3 cups peeled and diced butternut squash, • from a 1½ pound squash
⅛ teaspoon freshly ground black pepper
⅛ teaspoon Aleppo pepper or dried red pepper flakes
1 teaspoon honey or to taste

1. Soak the beans overnight in water to cover. The next day, drain, rinse and drain them again. Put them in large pot with 8 cups of water and bay leaves. Bring to a boil, cover and simmer until almost tender, 45-50 minutes. Add 1 tablespoon salt and cook 10 minutes more. Set aside.

2. Heat the oil in second large pot over medium heat. Add the onion, carrot, celery, parsnip, garlic and sage. Sauté until the vegetables have softened, about 10 minutes.

3. Add the squash and sauté about 10 minutes. Season with the remaining salt and peppers.

4. Purée 1 cup of beans with ¼ cup of their cooking water and add it to the vegetables. Add the beans, their water, bay leaves and honey. Simmer partly covered until the vegetables are completely tender, about 30 minutes more. Discard sage bundle and bay leaves.

• To peel the squash, cut the squash into halves and then into fourths. Discard the seeds. Use a vegetable peeler to peel each section down to the orange flesh.

Chicken Stock

Makes about 4 quarts

This rich stock can be a base for many soups. The chicken remains moist enough for salads or sandwiches.

About 10 pounds of chickens, quartered or in pieces
4 quarts cold water
4 carrots, scrubbed and cut into chunks
2 celery ribs with leaves
2 large onions, unpeeled, halved
1 parsnip, scrubbed and cut into chunks
2 garlic cloves, unpeeled, halved
1 teaspoon dried thyme
2 bay leaves
6 sprigs fresh parsley
12 peppercorns
6 whole cloves
1 unpeeled fresh tomato, optional

1. Put the chicken into a stockpot; add the cold water, making sure the chicken is immersed. Turn the heat to medium, partly cover the pot and cook until the stock begins to simmer.

2. When the stock is simmering, so-called "scum," which actually contains nutrients, will rise to the top. If you wish clear broth, skim it with a small strainer.

3. Add the remaining ingredients. Simmer partly covered about an hour, until the chicken is tender when pierced with a sharp knife. Remove the lid, take the pot off the heat and let the chicken cool in the stock, keeping it moist.

4. When the chicken is cool enough to handle, remove the skin and bones and return them to stockpot. Wrap the chicken well and refrigerate or freeze it for later use in sandwiches or chicken salad.

5. Let the stock simmer uncovered about 2 hours. (Do not allow it to boil. Boiling will disperse fat throughout the stock, making it cloudy.)

6. Pour the stock through a colander into a large clean bowl, discarding all solids. Then pour the stock through a strainer lined with a coffee filter or white paper towels into another bowl. Cool uncovered a short time and then refrigerate, uncovered. Cover only after stock is cold.

7. Remove any fat from the top and discard it. Freeze the stock in small increments to use for other soups.

To Skim or Not To Skim

Mother and I were in conflict on few issues, but skimming chicken stock was one of them. "You've got to skim it to get rid of the impurities," she would say. But Madelon Price, Professor Emeritus of Neurobiology at Washington University Medical School, says what Mother called impurities were actually different kinds of protein, collagen being one of them, that coagulate when heated and rise to the top. Roberta Duyff, author of *The American Dietetic Association's Complete Food and Nutrition Guide*, agrees that what people call "scum" is nutritious and need not be removed.

If, on the other hand, you want perfectly clear soup, skim it.

Chicken Soup

Serves 6.

6 cups chicken stock
Kosher salt and pepper to taste
2 carrots, sliced
1 cup fine noodles, ½ cup rice or ½ cup barley, optional
2 tablespoons minced fresh parsley

1. Bring the stock to a simmer. Season to taste with salt and pepper. Add the carrots and cook until they are tender.

2. Stir in the noodles, rice or barley. When tender, serve the soup garnished with parsley.

Turkey Stock

Makes about 7-8 cups

I bet the Puritans made turkey stock. What a waste not to.

1 carcass from a 12-15 pound roasted turkey
Cold water to cover
2 carrots, scrubbed
1 celery rib
2 onions, unpeeled, halved
2 garlic cloves, unpeeled, halved
1 bay leaf
½ teaspoon dried thyme
6 peppercorns

1. Put the turkey carcass in a large stockpot and add cold water to cover. Bring to a simmer.

2. Add the vegetables and seasonings. Simmer partly covered for 1½ hours.

3. Pour the stock through a colander into a large clean bowl, discarding skin, bones, seasonings and vegetables. Then pour it through a strainer, lined with a coffee filter or white paper towels, into another bowl. Cool uncovered a short time and then refrigerate, uncovered. Cover only when the stock is cold.

4. Remove and discard any fat from top and freeze the stock in small increments to use in place of chicken stock.

Note:
For a larger turkey, adjust the ingredients accordingly.

Summer Chowder

Makes 6-7 cups

This is a great vegetarian soup, especially when corn is at its best.

6 ears of corn
3 tablespoons extra virgin olive oil
1 medium onion, diced
2 celery ribs, peeled and diced
½ cup diced red bell pepper
1 jalapeño pepper, seeded and minced
1 tablespoon minced fresh ginger
1 garlic clove, minced
1½-2 tablespoons ground cumin
2 medium potatoes, peeled and diced
5½ cups milk
1½ teaspoons kosher salt
½ teaspoon freshly ground pepper
2 tablespoons butter

1. Remove the kernels from cobs by holding a cob on end over a clean towel. With a sharp knife, strip off the kernels from the middle of the cob down. Reverse the cob and strip off the rest of the kernels. By doing half a cob at a time, the kernels do not scatter as far. Break cobs in half; set everything aside.

2. Over medium heat, sauté the onion, celery and red bell pepper until soft, about 5 minutes. Add jalapeño, ginger, garlic and cumin. Sauté 3 minutes more.

3. Stir in the potatoes, milk and corn cobs. Simmer covered about 15 minutes or until the potatoes are tender. Discard the cobs.

4. Stir in the reserved corn kernels along with salt and pepper. Simmer until the corn is tender, about 3 minutes.

5. Remove about 2 cups of solids, purée them and return them to the soup to thicken it. Or purée the whole soup. Taste to adjust seasonings. Stir in the butter and serve.

Dirty Books: The Cook's Best Friends

If you find dirty books offensive, or if they entice you, or if you wonder why an essay devoted to dirty books has a place in a cookbook, let me come clean. The dirty books I refer to are those on your kitchen shelves and mine, the ones whose pages are splattered with gravy, shiny with olive oil and blotched with butter. They are the ones that put good food on the table. Hurrah for dirty books.

There are cookbook collectors, however, who prefer clean books. They have them stacked on bedside tables with little pieces of paper marking something that looks good. These collectors rarely cook and are quite content to find their pleasure in the pictures and descriptions. Indeed, some of these books are written so enticingly and are filled with such fine photographs, there is reason to read them if they never make it to the kitchen.

I admit that I hang onto some handsome books that remain pristine, like those from art museums and historical societies. And I never part with those I bought while traveling.

But if I use a book, I besmirch it. No pages covered with plastic wrap for me or one of those Lucite cookbook holders. I want no such barriers. Mother was that way. Her cookbooks, the well-used ones, fall open to properly besmirched pages that are like a trail of breadcrumbs, leading me to what she was cooking and thinking, as though she had left me notes.

My books, too, fall open to well-loved pages. Julia Child and Marcella Hazan's cookbooks, now held together by rubber bands, fall open to Julia's lentil soup and Marcella's minestrone.

Once a year, I sort my cookbooks and those that are too clean will be in the give-away pile. They will never be dirty enough for me.

Minestrone

Adapted from *Essentials of Classic Italian Cooking* by Marcella Hazan (Alfred A. Knopf, 1997)

Makes about 12 cups

Marcella says when making vegetable soup, if you put all the vegetables into the pot at once, they will taste like boiled vegetables. Doing it this way enhances the flavor of each vegetable.

½ cup extra virgin olive oil
3 tablespoons butter
1 cup sliced onion
1 cup diced carrots
1 cup diced celery
2 cups peeled, diced potatoes
¼ pound green beans, diced
1 pound zucchini, scrubbed and diced
½ pound green or Savoy cabbage, shredded
6 cups chicken broth or 2 cups canned beef broth plus 4 cups water
Crust from a 1-pound piece of Parmesan cheese scraped clean, optional but desirable. (Crusts can be purchased at some markets.)
⅔ cup canned Italian plum tomatoes, with their juice
1½ cups canned cannellini beans, drained and rinsed
Kosher salt and freshly ground pepper to taste
⅓ cup freshly grated Parmesan cheese

1. Put the oil, butter and onion in a large stockpot and cook over medium heat until onion is pale gold.

2. Add the carrots and cook 2 to 3 minutes, stirring once or twice.

3. Repeat the procedure with the celery, potatoes, green beans and zucchini, cooking each a few minutes and stirring.

4. Add the shredded cabbage and cook 6 minutes.

5. Add the broth, cheese crust, tomatoes, their juice and salt and pepper to taste. Simmer covered for at least 2½ hours.

6. Add the beans and cook 30 minutes more.

7. Remove the cheese crust, swirl in the Parmesan and add salt and pepper if necessary. (The cheese crust is the cook's prize.)

Lentil Soup

Serves 4-6

Esau traded his birthright for Jacob's bowl of lentil soup. Read *Genesis*, chapter 25, lines 30-34 to see why.

3 tablespoons butter, extra virgin olive oil or a combination
2 celery ribs, diced
1 medium carrot, diced
2 medium onions, diced
6 cups hot broth—chicken, beef, vegetable or hot water
1 bay leaf
¼ teaspoon thyme
¼ cup diced turnip
1½ cup washed lentils
2 teaspoons kosher salt

1 Heat the butter in a large saucepan; stir in the celery, carrots and onions and cook covered over low heat, stirring occasionally, until they are tender and just beginning to brown, about 10 minutes.

2. Add the hot broth, bay leaf, thyme, turnip, lentils and salt. Simmer partly covered for 1¼-1½ hours, until the lentils are tender. Remove the bay leaf.

3. Purée the soup if desired, adding more liquid if it seems too thick.

Spring Vegetable Soup

Serves 6-8

Sweet onions, baby turnips, fingerling potatoes and baby spinach make this a spring soup. But it's good made with the winter varieties, too.

3 tablespoons extra virgin olive oil
2 cups minced onions
1 cup sliced carrots
1 cup sliced celery
6 cups chicken broth or part chicken and beef broth, homemade or canned
½ cup tiny pasta, like alphabets or orzo
1 cup diced baby turnips
1 cup sliced fingerling potatoes, unpeeled
1 tomato, about ¾ cup, peeled, seeded and diced, or 1 cup canned tomatoes, with juices
1 bay leaf
1 teaspoon kosher salt
¼ teaspoon freshly ground pepper
2 ounces fresh baby spinach, about 4 cups

1. Put the oil in a heavy 3-quart pan. Add the onions, carrots and celery; sauté the vegetables about 8 minutes over medium heat, until they begin to soften.

2. Pour in the broth, pasta, turnips, potatoes, tomato, bay leaf, salt and pepper. Simmer partly covered about 1 hour or until the vegetables are tender. Remove the bay leaf.

3. To thicken the soup, purée 1 cup of the solids and return it to the soup.

4. To serve, bring the soup to a simmer. Add the spinach and continue cooking until the spinach wilts, about 2 minutes. Serve at once.

Simple Split Pea Soup with Mint

Makes about 8 cups

It's good served hot or cold.

2 cups green split peas, rinsed
1 medium onion, sliced
4 garlic cloves, peeled and crushed
1 potato, about 8 ounces, peeled and cubed
6 cups chicken broth, homemade or canned
4 sprigs fresh mint bundled with kitchen twine
Kosher salt and freshly ground white pepper to taste
Fresh mint leaves to garnish

1. Combine the peas with the onion, garlic, potato and broth. Simmer covered 30 minutes. Add the mint and simmer 10 minutes more or until the peas and potatoes are tender. Discard the mint.

2. Purée the soup. Season to taste with salt and pepper. For cold soup, chill overnight, adding more seasoning if needed. (Cold soups require more seasoning than hot.)

3. To serve, garnish with fresh mint leaves.

Sweet Onion and Potato Soup

Serves 6-8

This simple vegetarian soup has variations.

1½ pounds Vidalia or other sweet onions, peeled and chopped, about 4 cups
1½ pounds baking potatoes, peeled and chopped, about 4 cups
2 garlic cloves, peeled
5 cups water
1½-2 teaspoons kosher salt
¼ teaspoon white pepper
2 tablespoons butter
1 cup cooked diced carrots, cooked sliced sugar snaps, cooked broccoli
   florets, optional
¼ cup freshly grated Parmesan cheese
Chopped chives or parsley to garnish

1. Put the onions, potatoes and garlic in a saucepan with the water. Bring to a boil, add salt and pepper and simmer partly covered 20 to 30 minutes or until the vegetables are tender.

2. Do not drain. Purée everything in a food processor. Strain the soup to remove any lumps. Refrigerate if serving later.

3. To serve, reheat the soup and add the butter. Add the cooked carrots, sugar snaps or broccoli. Taste to check seasoning.

4. Sprinkle with the Parmesan cheese and chopped chives or parsley.

The Story of Stone Soup

In the mid-thirties, when America was in the Great Depression, *The Story of Stone Soup* was in my third grade *Reader*. The *Reader* is long gone, but not the story.

A long time ago, an old man was walking down a country road on his way to the next town. The night was dark, the moon hidden by rain clouds, and he was tired, wet and hungry. At last, he came to a large house where light was shining from the kitchen windows. He knocked on the door.

"You can come in and dry yourself by the kitchen fire," Cook told the old man who stood at the door, shivering. "But I can't give you anything to eat. We have just enough for ourselves."

He sat on a wooden stool next to the fire whose radiance lit up the room. Its warmth began to dry his wet clothes. "Have you ever heard of Stone Soup?" he asked.

"Don't be silly," she said. "You can't make soup out of a stone."

"I can," he said. "Give me a pot of water and I will make Stone Soup."

Cook brought out her black iron soup kettle full of water, and the old man hung it on the hook over the fire. Then, he took a smooth white stone the size of a small potato from his pocket and slipped it into the pot. Soon, the pot began to steam. The old man tasted the soup.

"This is the best Stone Soup I have ever made," he said. "But if I had a potato, it would be even better."

Cook was interested. "I can spare a potato," she said.

He added the potato to the pot, and after a bit, tasted it again. "This is the best Stone Soup I have ever made," he said. " If only I had an onion, it would be even better."

Cook, growing more and more curious, gave him an onion. "Mmmm," he said after one taste. "Now if I had a turnip and a carrot, this would indeed be the best Stone Soup I ever made."

Cook gave him what he asked, and then, getting into the spirit of the soup, brought him some salt and pepper. By now, the aroma of the soup simmering over the fire filled her kitchen.

Once more, the old man tasted the soup. "This is the best Stone Soup I have ever made," he said, "and it's ready to eat."

He and Cook sat at the kitchen table and ate bowl after bowl of Stone Soup until it was all gone. Cook even found some bread for them to wipe their bowls clean.

This is the most wonderful soup I have ever tasted," she said. "And to think you made it with a stone."

The old man wiped the stone dry and presented it to Cook. "Now I shall have Stone Soup whenever I wish," she said.

By this time, a bright moon lit up the road, and the old man went on his way, warm and dry, filled with the magic of good soup.

Stone Soup

Makes 6-8 cups

For unusual ingredients, please see *The Story of Stone Soup.*

1 smooth clean white stone, optional
2 cups peeled and diced potatoes
2 cups chopped onion
1½ cups diced turnip
1½ cups sliced carrot
4 cups water
1½ teaspoons kosher salt
½ teaspoon pepper
1 (15-ounce) can cannellini beans, optional
Butter

1. Combine the optional stone with the potatoes, onion, turnip, carrots and water. Add salt and pepper. Bring to a boil and simmer partly covered 30 minutes.

2. Purée one cup of solids to thicken the soup.

3. If Cook has a can of cannellini beans, rinse and drain them and stir them into the soup. Taste to adjust seasoning. Remove the optional stone.

4. To serve, garnish each bowl with a teaspoon of butter.

Note:
There were no beans or butter in the original story, but they add body to the soup and enhance its flavor.

Tomato Soup

Makes 5-6 cups

The flavor depends on the flavor of the tomatoes. Serve the soup hot or cold.

3-4 pounds ripe excellent tasting tomatoes
3 tablespoons olive oil
2 large onions, sliced
1 garlic clove, minced
3 sprigs flat-leaf parsley
5 basil leaves
1 potato, about 6 ounces, peeled and diced
2-3 teaspoons kosher salt
½ teaspoon white pepper
1 teaspoon sugar, optional
½ teaspoon cayenne pepper, optional
Sour cream and fresh basil leaves to garnish

1. Drop the tomatoes into boiling water for 10 seconds. Remove them with a slotted spoon. Peel at once or refrigerate them to peel later.

2. Sauté the onions on medium heat until they are tender and translucent, about 8-10 minutes. Add the garlic and sauté 2 minutes more.

3. Bundle the parsley and basil together with kitchen twine. Stir into the onions. Cut the peeled tomatoes into chunks and add to the onions. Add the potato. Simmer covered about 30 minutes, stirring occasionally, until the potato is tender. Discard the parsley and basil bundle.

4. Purée in a food processor. For an elegant soup, strain it, pressing all the liquid out of the solids. Season to taste with salt and pepper. Add sugar if the soup is too tart. Add cayenne pepper and top with a dollop of sour cream and fresh basil leaves.

Wild Mushroom Soup with Barley

Makes about 12 cups

This unusual soup has a distinct earthy flavor.

2 ounces dried porcini mushrooms
3 cups warm tap water
2 pounds fresh white mushrooms
2 roma tomatoes
6 tablespoons extra virgin olive oil
1 cup minced onion
¼ cup minced fresh parsley
6 cups chicken stock, homemade or canned
½ cup barley
2 teaspoons dried tarragon leaves
Kosher salt and freshly ground pepper to taste
Fresh parsley or tarragon to garnish

1. Soak the porcini in warm tap water for at least thirty minutes. Set a strainer lined with a white paper towel or coffee filter over a bowl. Drain the soaked porcini. Reserve soaking liquid. Wash the porcini thoroughly under cold running water to get rid of any sand or grit. Chop them coarsely and set aside.

2. Rinse the fresh mushrooms quickly under cold running water. Dry them on terrycloth towels and thinly slice them. A food processor works well here. Set them aside.

3. Dip the tomatoes into boiling water for 10 seconds. Peel and dice, saving their juices. Set them aside.

4. Put the oil and onion in a heavy pan. Turn the heat to medium and cook, stirring frequently until the onion is pale gold. Add the porcini, their soaking liquid, tomatoes, their juices and parsley. Cook uncovered over medium to high heat until almost all liquid has evaporated.

5. Add the fresh mushrooms, cover and cook on medium heat until the mushrooms have released their liquid. Uncover the pan, raise the heat to medium high and cook until almost all the liquid has evaporated.

6. Stir in the stock, barley, tarragon, salt and pepper. Simmer covered about 35-40 minutes or until the barley is tender.

7. For slightly thicker soup, purée 2 cups of the solids. To serve, garnish with minced fresh parsley or tarragon.

Asparagus Soup

Serves 4

1 pound asparagus
4 cups boiling water
1 cup onions, diced
2 tablespoons butter
1 garlic clove, minced
¼ cup rice
Kosher salt and freshly ground pepper to taste
Sour cream, optional
2 tablespoons minced fresh parsley

1. Wash the asparagus. Cut off the tips. Drop them into the boiling water. Have a bowl of iced water ready. After 3 minutes, scoop the tips out the water and drop them into the iced water. When chilled, drain, dry them and slice them lengthwise if desired. Set them aside to garnish the soup. Reserve the water in which the tips were cooked.

2. Sauté the onions in the butter about 7-8 minutes on medium heat, until tender and translucent. Don't allow them to brown. Stir in the garlic and sauté 2 minutes more.

3. Add the rice and stir to coat the grains. Add the water the tips were cooked in; simmer covered for 15 minutes. Cut the spears into ½-inch pieces. Add them and cook about 5 minutes more or until the asparagus and rice are tender.

4. Purée the soup. Add salt and pepper to taste. Garnish with the reserved asparagus tips and sour cream. Sprinkle with the parsley.

My Gazpacho

Makes about 9 cups

The better the tomatoes, the better the gazpacho.

1 red or yellow bell pepper, seeded and roughly chopped
3 celery ribs, roughly chopped
2 medium cucumbers, peeled and roughly chopped, seeding optional
1 large onion, quartered
1 garlic clove, chopped
2 tablespoons chopped fresh parsley
2 tablespoons good quality red wine vinegar or sherry vinegar
3 pounds fresh good tasting tomatoes, peeled • and quartered
¼ cup extra virgin olive oil
2 teaspoons kosher salt or to taste
Freshly ground pepper to taste
½ teaspoon ground cumin, or more to taste

1. A food processor works well with this recipe. Process the pepper, celery, cucumber, onion, garlic and parsley, coarse or fine, as you wish. Add the vinegar. Transfer to a large bowl.

2. Add the tomatoes to the processor. With the motor running, pour in the oil. Add to the bowl.

3. Season to taste with salt, pepper, and cumin. Refrigerate overnight if possible.

• To peel tomatoes, drop them into boiling water for 10 seconds. Remove them with a slotted spoon and peel immediately or refrigerate them to peel later.

Cold Cucumber Soup with Mint

Serves 6-8

Cucumber Soup could have been around in Egypt in Biblical times. Read *Numbers*, Chapter 11, line 5: On their journey through the wilderness, the Israelites complained because all they had to eat was manna. They recalled with pleasure "the cucumbers... and the leeks, and the onions, and the garlic" they ate in Egypt.

That's the start of Cucumber Soup. Add olive oil, wild mint, salt, vinegar and yogurt, all readily available in Biblical days. Making fresh milk into yogurt was the way to preserve it.

3 pounds cucumbers, peeled and halved lengthwise
1 tablespoon kosher salt, divided
½ cup sweet onion or 8 scallions, chopped
3 tablespoons extra virgin olive oil
4 teaspoons red wine vinegar
2 tablespoons chopped fresh mint
2 cups plain yogurt, whole milk or low fat
Freshly ground black pepper
½ teaspoon garlic powder
Fresh mint leaves to garnish

1. Set a colander over a bowl. With a spoon, scoop the cucumber seeds into the colander. Sprinkle them with 1 teaspoon salt and set aside to drain about 15 minutes. Discard the seeds. Reserve the liquid.

2. Coarsely chop the cucumbers and transfer them to a blender or food processor. Add the onion, olive oil, vinegar and mint. Process until blended.

3. Add the yogurt, remaining salt, pepper, garlic powder and liquid from the drained cucumber seeds. Blend until smooth. Chill. Garnish with fresh mint leaves.

Almost Homemade Beet Borscht

Serves 4

Back in the days of our first apartment, without air conditioning, we ate a lot of cold borscht followed by cold watermelon.

1 quart prepared borscht with beets
Juice of ½ lemon
½ teaspoon salt
2 egg yolks
Sour cream or plain yogurt, to garnish
Sprigs of fresh herbs, to garnish

1. Pour the borsht into a saucepan. Season it with the lemon juice and salt and bring it to a simmer.

2. In a small metal bowl, beat the egg yolks with a fork. Whisk a teaspoon of the simmering borsht into the yolks. Whisk rapidly to cool the borsht and prevent it from cooking the eggs.

3. Add another spoonful and then another, whisking rapidly the whole time. When the egg yolks are fairly warm, stir them into the pot of simmering borscht.

4. Simmer 3 minutes more to thoroughly cook the eggs. Cool and refrigerate.

5. To serve, garnish with dollops of sour cream and sprigs of fresh herbs.

Garlic Croutons

Adapted from *How to Cook Everything* by Mark Bittman (Macmillan, 1998)

Makes about 2 cups

These croutons make soups even better. Bittman writes, "You'll never use purchased croutons again."

4 tablespoons extra virgin olive oil, butter or a combination
4 garlic cloves, peeled
4-6 slices of French or Italian bread, cut into cubes, crusts optional
Kosher salt to taste

1. Heat the olive oil in a large skillet on medium-low heat. Add the garlic, turning often, until it is lightly browned. Remove the garlic, which is now pleasantly mild; save to add to a salad or soup.

2. Turn the heat to medium and toast the bread in the oil, turning the cubes occasionally, until brown all over. Remove and sprinkle lightly with salt. Set aside uncovered and use them the day you make them.

Salads

Black Circle Series, *detail*
Waterless Lithography. 10" x 10".

Deli Delight

On a trip to New York several years ago, we made Carnegie Delicatessen our first stop. Seated at our table (or we at theirs, because everyone shares tables at Carnegie's) was a couple from Birmingham, Alabama. They told us their travel agent told them to go to Carnegie's.

Without even glancing at the menu, we ordered one hot pastrami sandwich on Jewish rye and coleslaw. We knew from experience that the charge for splitting an order was worth it.

The couple from Birmingham studied the menu. Trying to be hospitable, we suggested they split a pastrami sandwich as we were doing. "No," they said. "We want sliced chicken sandwiches on white bread with French fries."

While waiting for our lunches, we consumed the pickles on our end of the table. We could have eaten theirs also, because they weren't. Our sandwich arrived, a mountain of glistening, moist, succulent hot pastrami on slices of real Jewish rye bread, without parsley, lemon slices or watercress—enough meat and bread to feed the two of us handsomely. With it was a small platter of coleslaw, meant for one but enough for two. The slaw was the right mix of vinegar, sugar, salt and mayonnaise.

Our neighbors' sandwiches arrived also, with chicken piled as high as our pastrami, on thin slices of white bread, each order with a small mountain of fries. They looked appalled at the quantity, but we had no sympathy for them. In the first place, they should have taken our advice about splitting a sandwich, and second, they should have ordered pastrami.

Passing up pastrami in New York City is like visiting St. Louis without seeing the Arch. Their travel agent should have told them.

Almost Carnegie Coleslaw

Serves 8

We loved this slaw at the Carnegie Deli in New York. When we returned to St.Louis, I phoned the restaurant for the recipe. The manager said he couldn't give it to me, probably because he knew it only in huge quantities, but he could give me the ingredients. A little sleuthing in cookbooks produced Almost Carnegie Coleslaw.

8 cups (about 1½ pounds) shredded cabbage
1 medium carrot, shredded
1 small sweet onion, minced
1 cup mayonnaise (can be part reduced fat mayonnaise)
⅓ cup plus 1 tablespoon cider vinegar
1 tablespoon water
½ cup sugar
½ teaspoon kosher salt
⅛ teaspoon black pepper
Optional: 1 diced red or yellow bell pepper, 1 small diced unpeeled zucchini, ¼ cup
  minced fresh parsley

1. If using purchased shredded cabbage, rinse it with cold water, let it drain and eliminate the tablespoon of water.

2. If purchasing whole cabbage, shred 1½ pounds of it in the food processor. Add the carrot and onion. Empty into a large bowl.

3. Without washing the bowl of the food processor, process the mayonnaise, vinegar, water, sugar, salt and pepper. Taste to check the seasoning. Pour over the slaw and toss. Toss in the bell peppers, zucchini and parsley if desired. Keeps refrigerated up to 5 days.

Salad for a Crowd

Use these guidelines to make salad for any size crowd.

Vinaigrette, about 3 cups
2 garlic cloves
1 teaspoon kosher salt
2 tablespoons fresh minced parsley
1 cup red wine vinegar or sherry vinegar
2 tablespoons minced shallots
2 teaspoons Dijon mustard
Freshly ground black pepper to taste
2 cups extra virgin olive oil
1 teaspoon sugar, optional

1. Mash the garlic with salt to form a paste. Put it in a blender, food processor or jar with a lid. Add the parsley, vinegar, shallots, mustard and pepper. Blend until smooth.

2. Add the oil in a slow steady stream and blend well. Taste and adjust seasoning, adding sugar, more salt or oil. Refrigerate up to 5 days. Bring to room temperature and shake well before using.

Salad ingredients

1. Allow about 1-ounce (about 2 cups) per person of washed and dried greens such as mixed salad greens, baby spinach, arugula.

2. Allow ¼-½ cup per person of any the following: cocktail tomatoes, red onion rings, sliced cucumbers, shredded carrots, shredded red or white cabbage, scallions.

3. To prepare the salad, combine salad ingredients in a large bowl. Toss with just enough vinaigrette to make everything glisten. Serve at once.

Italian Tossed Salad

Serves 6

Italians do not use prepared salad dressings. Our waiter at the Villa Cipriani Hotel in Asolo, Italy combined a variety of greens with anything we wished (see list below) in a large bowl. He gently tossed the salad with salt, freshly ground black pepper and enough extra virgin olive oil to make the ingredients glisten. He sprinkled on drops of excellent red wine vinegar, gently tossed again, and served the salad immediately. When we do it this way at home, guests often say, "What a good salad dressing."

2 carrots, peeled and shredded
1 fennel bulb, thinly sliced
4 scallions, thinly sliced
1 red or yellow bell pepper, diced
1 cucumber, peeled and thinly sliced
6 ounces (about 12 cups) salad greens like Boston, arugula, Bibb, romaine, spinach
   or red leaf, washed, dried and torn into bite size pieces
Kosher salt and freshly ground pepper to taste
Extra virgin olive oil
1 large tomato, cut into narrow wedges
Red wine or sherry vinegar

1. Combine the selected vegetables and salad greens in a large bowl.

2. Toss gently with salt and pepper and enough olive oil to make everything glisten.

3. Add the tomato. Sprinkle with the wine vinegar. Toss gently. Taste and adjust the seasoning if necessary. Serve at once.

Quickles

Serves 4

This old family recipe was one of Mother's favorites.

2 large cucumbers, peeled, leaving a little of the green
1 large onion
1 tablespoon kosher salt
1 cup sugar
1 cup cider vinegar
½ cup water
1 tablespoon dill weed, optional

1. Slice the cucumbers and onions in a food processor. Put them in a bowl and sprinkle with the salt. Cover with ice cubes and put a plate on top to weigh them down. Cover with plastic wrap so your refrigerator won't smell like onions. Refrigerate several hours or overnight.

2. To prepare the Quickles, drain the cucumbers and onions in a colander. With your hands, squeeze them to remove all liquid. Do three "squeezings," from colander to bowl and back again.

3. Combine the sugar, vinegar, water and optional dill weed in a saucepan. Bring to a boil, simmer 2 minutes and pour over the cucumbers immediately. Cover and refrigerate. Quickles can stay several weeks in the refrigerator.

4. To serve, line a bowl with lettuce leaves or purple kale and fill it with Quickles. Serve with a slotted spoon.

A House Divided

Billy and I are a house divided when it comes to lettuce. I love the leafy lettuces available all year in the stores and early summer at farmers' markets: peppery arugula, curly and mildly bitter frisée, sweet mild oak leaf, dark green nutty mâche and red, slightly bitter radicchio. For my favorite salad, I toss them all together, with Vidalia onion rings, kosher salt, freshly ground pepper and extra virgin olive oil (enough to make the leaves shiny) followed by a few drops of high-quality red wine vinegar. If there are good tomatoes and avocados, they go in, too. Served immediately, there is nothing finer!

Billy calls my salad "weeds." His favorite is a wedge of iceberg lettuce with Russian Thousand Island dressing cascading over it. And were you to query your friends, especially the male ones, you would discover a definite preference for iceberg lettuce. You can't even get it at a farmers' market, at least not here. It comes from California, and its real name is head lettuce. It was called iceberg because of the mounds of ice needed to ship it.

Growing up in Belleville, Illinois, I ate a lot of iceberg lettuce, either cut into wedges as described above or cut up with cucumbers, sweet onions, radishes and tomatoes tossed with my mother's homemade dressing. (We ate it cut up until my sister returned from college with the news that lettuce should be torn, not cut, into bite-sized pieces.) The only other lettuce I ever saw was at Girl Scout banquets where pale green leaf lettuce was tossed with sweet vinegar and bacon grease.

We no longer argue about whose salad is better. He accepts my "weeds," and I have become quite attached to a wedge of iceberg lettuce topped with Russian Thousand Island Dressing. I do remind him, however, that my favorite dark green lettuces contain healthy minerals and vitamins, while his crisp but pale iceberg lettuce has little or no food value.

"It's all in where you place your values," he says.

Iceberg Lettuce with Russian Thousand Island Dressing

Makes about 1½ cups of dressing

Zestier than plain Thousand Island, it's good on sandwiches, too.

1 head iceberg lettuce
1 cup mayonnaise
¼ cup chili sauce or ketchup, or more to taste
1 hard-boiled egg, finely chopped
1 tablespoon fresh bottled horseradish, or more to taste
1 teaspoon Worcestershire sauce
1 tablespoon minced fresh onion
1 tablespoon minced fresh parsley
Kosher salt and freshly ground pepper to taste
Extras: slices of tomato, cucumber, scallions, avocado, chicken, roast beef, hard-
   boiled eggs

1. The day you plan to serve the salad, remove any wilted leaves from the lettuce. Rinse the whole head under cold running water. Wrap in clean towels to dry. Refrigerate until serving.

2. Combine mayonnaise, chili sauce, egg, horseradish, Worcestershire sauce, onion, parsley, salt and pepper in a food processor or a jar with a good lid. Blend well. Taste to adjust seasonings. Cover and refrigerate up to three days.

3. Cut iceberg into wedges. Add extras as desired. Drizzle on the dressing.

The Best House Salad

Serves 6

Adapted from a popular St. Louis restaurant, it's good with broiled chicken, salmon or hot dogs and can be served nicely on the same plate.

1 head iceberg lettuce
1 head romaine lettuce
⅔ cup extra virgin olive oil
⅓ cup red wine vinegar
1-1¼ teaspoons kosher salt
¼-½ teaspoon freshly ground pepper
1 cup artichoke hearts, drained and chopped
1 cup thinly sliced red onions
1 cup pimentos, drained and diced
⅔ cup freshly grated Parmesan cheese

1. The day you plan to serve the salad, remove any wilted leaves from the iceberg lettuce. Rinse the whole head under cold running water. Wrap in clean towels to dry. Refrigerate

2. Wash and dry the romaine. Refrigerate it in a zip lock bag.

3. Combine the olive oil, vinegar, salt and pepper in a jar with a good lid. Shake well and set aside at room temperature.

4. Shortly before serving the salad, tear the iceberg into pieces. There will be about 12 cups. Put it into a large salad bowl.

5. Tear the romaine leaves into thirds, enough to make about 3 cups. Add to the salad bowl.

6. Add the artichokes, onions and pimentos.

7. Toss everything with all of the vinaigrette. Toss again with the Parmesan cheese and serve immediately.

French Potato Salad

Inspired by Julia Child

Serves 4

Vinaigrette
1 small garlic clove
2-3 pinches kosher salt
½ cup red wine or sherry vinegar
1 shallot, minced
1 teaspoon Dijon mustard
Freshly ground black pepper to taste
1 cup extra virgin olive oil
½ teaspoon sugar, optional

Potato Salad
2 pounds boiling potatoes
½ teaspoons kosher salt
Freshly ground black pepper
2 tablespoons minced shallots
4 tablespoons white wine
4 tablespoons chicken stock
Lettuce to line the serving platter

Vinaigrette
1. Mash the garlic with the salt to form a paste. Put it in a blender, food processor or jar with a lid. Add the vinegar, shallot, mustard and pepper. Blend until smooth.

2. Add the oil in a slow steady stream and blend well. Taste and adjust seasoning, adding sugar, more salt or oil. Refrigerate up to 5 days. Shake well before using.

Potato Salad
1. Steam the potatoes until tender when pierced with a small knife.

2. While hot, peel them if desired, cut in half if large, and slice in ⅜-inch slices.

3. Sprinkle with salt and pepper. Toss gently with the shallots, wine and stock. Let sit about 5 minutes to allow the potatoes to absorb the liquid.

4. Toss with 5-6 tablespoons of the vinaigrette. Refrigerate until about 30 minutes before serving

5. Taste the salad to adjust seasonings, adding sugar, more salt or oil. Serve on a platter lined with lettuce.

Note:
1. To serve 12 generously, triple the potato salad but only double the vinaigrette.

2. This vinaigrette is good with cold string beans, cold asparagus and green salad.

Slightly Different Egg Salad

Makes about 2 cups

6 eggs
¼ cup extra virgin olive oil
1 medium yellow onion or 6 scallions, chopped, about ½ cup
2 tablespoons chopped fresh parsley or dill
1 teaspoon kosher salt
Freshly ground black pepper to taste
Garnish: lettuce, paprika, tomato, cucumber or black olives

1. Place the eggs in a single layer in a saucepan and add water to cover by 1 inch. Bring to a full boil over high heat. Remove from the heat, cover and let stand 11 minutes. Drain the eggs and chill them under cold running water. (Chilling makes them easier to peel.)

2. Chop the eggs or mash them. Combine them with the remaining ingredients. For chunkier texture, stir until the mixture just holds together; for a smoother salad, blend well. Cover and refrigerate.

3. Garnish as desired and serve with crackers, matzo, dark bread or challah.

Country Club Chicken Salad

Serves 3-4

I tasted this chicken salad at a meeting at a country club. The chef sent me the recipe.

1 pound cooked chicken
2 celery ribs
1 tablespoon extra virgin olive oil
Kosher salt and freshly ground pepper to taste
1 tablespoon fresh lemon or lime juice
½ cup mayonnaise (can be part reduced fat mayonnaise)
2-3 tablespoons Durkee Famous Sauce
2 tablespoons Sugar Roasted Nuts to garnish

1. Cut the chicken and celery into ½-inch dice. Toss with the olive oil, salt and pepper to taste and lemon juice.

2. Whisk the mayonnaise with 2 tablespoons of the Durkee Famous Sauce. Toss with the chicken and celery. Taste to adjust the seasonings.

3. To serve, top with the nuts.

Note:
For variation, add one or more of the following: unpeeled diced apple, sliced grapes, zest of 1 lemon and 1 lime, golden raisins, pinch of chopped cilantro.

Farmer's Chop Suey

Serves 4

When I was a child growing up in Belleville, sour cream was part of our diet. Every week, Mrs. Croop delivered to our back door a blue glass quart Mason jar filled with thick sour cream. (Another farmer brought white asparagus and another, chickens and eggs. That's the way it was in a small town in the thirties.) As long as there were good tomatoes, cucumbers and radishes, Mother served Farmer's Chop Suey all summer.

2 medium cucumbers, peeled and thinly sliced, about 2 cups
2 scallions, sliced
2 tomatoes cut into bite-sized chunks, about 1 cup
6 red radishes, sliced, about 1 cup
Kosher salt and freshly ground pepper to taste
1 cup sour cream

1. Combine the cucumbers, scallions, tomatoes and radishes. Season to taste with salt and pepper.

2. Fold in the sour cream and serve at once.

Note:
You can use light sour cream or half sour cream and half yogurt.

Grains

Stripes, *detail*
Waterless Lithography. 19" x 19" .

Marcella Hazan: Queen of Italian Cuisine

Marcella Hazan is the author of six Italian cookbooks, plus a forthcoming memoir. With the publication of each book, her popularity has increased, perhaps because she ladles out her philosophy: "Since eating is something we must do to live, why not spend time making it enjoyable."

A few years ago, Marcella and her husband Victor, an expert on Italian wines, left their apartment on the top floor of a sixteenth-century palazzo in Venice, Italy and moved to a condo on the beach in Longboat Key, Florida, near their son and his family. The first thing they did was remodel the kitchen, angling the cook top to give her a view of the Gulf of Mexico while she cooks and changing the large refrigerator for a small one, because she markets daily.

For Marcella, memorable Italian meals begin with marketing. "I make my menu around vegetables and I buy only what's fresh," she says. "Meat and fish are always there."

Marcella began her professional career as a scientist. With doctorate degrees in geology, paleontology and biology, she spent most of her time in the laboratory. She prepared wonderful meals even then, however, because she always knew how food should look and taste—her grandmother and mother were good cooks—and because it was part of her Italian heritage.

"Victor liked to eat very much," she says of their newlywed days in the United States. "And it is encouraging to cook for someone like that. You always want to do better and better."

American friends who dined in their home encouraged her to write her first cookbook, and she began her second career.

She finds Americans curious about food and willing to try something new, but they do not give food the priority it has in Italy.

"Americans talk a lot about food, but actually, they don't do much," she says. "They say they don't have time to cook, but it's not true. They spend their time on other things. They say, 'I cook on weekends.' And I say, 'What do you do the rest of the week? Starve? Eat out? If they just cook a chop and make a tomato salad, they can eat nicely."

Pasta With Pesto Sauce

Adapted from *Essentials of Classic Italian Cooking* by Marcella Hazan (Alfred A. Knopf, 1997)

Serves 8 as a first course or side dish, 4 as a main course

Grow your own basil and you can squirrel away this sauce all summer. Freeze it without the cheeses and softened butter.

2 cups tightly packed fresh basil leaves, well washed in cold water and patted dry
½ cup extra virgin olive oil
3 tablespoons pine nuts
2 garlic cloves, chopped fine before putting them in the processor
1 teaspoon kosher salt
½ cup freshly grated Parmesan cheese
2 tablespoons freshly grated Pecorino Romano cheese
3 tablespoons butter softened to room temperature
1½ pounds pasta

1. Put the basil, olive oil, pine nuts, garlic and salt in a food processor and process to a uniform creamy consistency.

2. Transfer to a bowl, and mix in the 2 grated cheeses by hand. Mix in the softened butter.

3. Cook the pasta in a big pot of boiling salted water until it is tender but firm to the bite. Drain the pasta into a large bowl, reserving ½ cup of the cooking water.

4. Toss the pasta with the pesto sauce, diluting it slightly with a tablespoon or two of the hot water in which the pasta was cooked.

Running Out of Spaghetti

Our first apartment was on the third floor in a building on Washington Avenue, across from an old folk's home, where we depended on the air-cooling machines on the top of the Varsity Theater across the alley to cool us, where we had plenty of hot water but little or no heat and where I once beat a mouse to death with my broom. All our friends lived in such conditions, including the mouse, and we would gather to laugh about it. (Of course, our mothers didn't.)

Billy and I decided to have our families to dinner, perhaps to let them know that we were living well, after all. Mothers and fathers, siblings, aunts, uncles and cousins, totalling twenty. We kept our menu simple—spaghetti with meat sauce, salad, bread and cookies—a nice Sunday supper for newlyweds to put out, right? But outside of poisoning the guests, the dinner was a nightmare: we ran out of spaghetti.

Now, even though that apartment on Washington Avenue had its drawbacks, it was well located. Exactly one half block away, on the corner of Delmar and Melville, was a saloon that always had spaghetti. So Billy ran quietly down our back steps (thirty seven of them) to the corner saloon, refilled our casserole and ran back up the steps without anyone knowing.

That night, we learned an important lesson in entertaining: always plan more food than you think you need. And you might as well buy your spaghetti at the corner saloon, because it's possible that no one will know the difference.

Baked Pasta with Tomato Sauce and Cheeses

Serves 6-8

This easy do-ahead dish is especially nutritious when made with whole-wheat pasta. I rarely cook with prepared foods, but I make an exception here. There are so many good pasta tomato sauces on grocery shelves that will enhance this baked pasta. Find a sauce you like and keep it in your pantry.

1 tablespoon kosher salt
1 pound pasta such as penne or ziti
2-3 cups purchased pasta tomato sauce
8 ounces fresh mozzarella cheese, packed in water, drained and grated, divided
1½ cups grated Swiss cheese, divided

1. Preheat the oven to 400 degrees. Grease a 9 x 13-inch baking dish. Set aside.

2. Bring 4 quarts water to a boil. Add the salt and pasta. Cook uncovered until the pasta is firm and slightly underdone. Drain.

3. Combine the pasta and tomato sauce. Pour half of it into the prepared baking dish, sprinkle with half the mozzarella and half the Swiss. Top with remaining pasta and sprinkle with remaining cheeses. (The dish can be assembled early and refrigerated. Bring it to room temperature one hour before baking.)

4. Bake on an upper rack in the oven for 20 minutes or until the top starts to brown. Serve at once.

Summer Bow Ties

Serves 6-8

4 ears fresh corn
½ cup extra virgin olive oil, divided
½ pound roma tomatoes
1 tablespoon kosher salt plus more to taste
1 pound bow tie pasta
Freshly ground pepper to taste
2 tablespoons balsamic vinegar
2 tablespoons fresh lemon juice
½ cup sliced scallions

1. Remove the kernels from cobs by holding a cob on end over a clean towel. With a sharp knife, strip off the kernels from the middle of the cob down. Reverse the cob and strip off the rest of the kernels. By doing half a cob at a time, the kernels do not scatter as far.

2. Put 2 tablespoons of the oil in a skillet that can take high heat, like cast iron. Turn the heat to high. Add the corn and cook, shaking the pan or stirring occasionally, until the corn is lightly charred, about 5-8 minutes. Set aside.

3. Core the tomatoes, halve them and remove the seeds. Dice and set aside.

4. Bring 4 quarts of water to a boil. Stir in a tablespoon of salt and the pasta. Cook uncovered 10-11 minutes until the bow ties are tender but firm. Drain.

5. In a large bowl, toss the bow ties with the remaining 6 tablespoons of oil, salt and pepper to taste. Stir in the vinegar and lemon juice. Add the corn, tomatoes and scallions. Toss again and taste to adjust seasonings. Serve at room temperature.

Pasta with Basil and Fresh Vegetables

Serves 2-4

This fresh-tasting pasta can be served hot or at room temperature.

1 tablespoon kosher salt
2 cups bite-size cauliflower florets
2 cups bite-size broccoli florets
¼ cup extra virgin olive oil
¼ cup chopped fresh basil
1 medium red onion, thinly sliced
1 small zucchini, about 5-6 ounces, scrubbed and thinly sliced
1 red bell pepper, seeded and cut into 1-inch squares
Kosher salt and freshly ground pepper to taste
4 ounces fusilli or macaroni
¼ cup freshly grated Parmesan cheese

1. Have a large bowl of ice water ready. Bring a large pot of water to a boil. Stir in the salt, and when the water returns to a boil, drop in the cauliflower. Boil it about 2 minutes. Remove it with a slotted spoon and chill it in the ice water. Do the same with the broccoli. Drain the vegetables and dry them on a large terrycloth towel.

2. If you are not preparing the pasta immediately, wrap the chilled vegetables and refrigerate them.

3. Add the oil and basil to a large skillet. Stir over medium high heat for 1 minute. Add the onion and sauté it for 1 minute. Add the zucchini and red pepper. Sauté them for 1 minute.

4. Stir in the cauliflower and broccoli. Cook and stir about 2-3 minutes or until everything is heated through but still crisp. Season to taste with salt and pepper.

5. Cook the pasta until firm but not soft. Scoop out a cup of the pasta cooking water and set it aside. Drain the pasta and toss it with the vegetables. If the pasta seems dry, add a tablespoon of the reserved pasta water. Toss with the Parmesan cheese and serve.

A Passover Memory

Jews all over the world celebrate the first night of Passover with a Seder, a feast commemorating the exodus of the Israelites from Egypt. I remember a particular Seder during the Second World War, when I was about fourteen. I recall my parents, my sister and brother and my grandparents from Arkansas seated at our dining room table in our house in Belleville. But there were also Sergeant Bloom and Private First Class Cohen, young men barely out of their teens, and Miss Langer and Miss Reese, as my father with old-fashioned courtesy called the servicewomen who were our guests, also. I know their names because my father wrote them down in the Haggadah, the book that relates the story of Passover. It was 1943.

In the springs that followed, Dad recorded names of more soldiers. But with the end of the war, Sergeant Bloom and Private First Class Cohen gave way to people new to Belleville, to college friends, to the schoolteacher who had recently lost her parents. It had become a family tradition to share our Seder with others.

Passover is a time of many traditions, the most celebrated being the exodus of the Israelites from Egypt. But before there was an exodus, spring—with its crop of new goats and lambs and the first grain harvest—was reason enough for an annual celebration called Pesach. Some years after the exodus, the two spring holidays became one, and Passover, or Pesach, became the festival of both deliverance and renewal.

In some homes, Seders last several hours, but in my parents' home, the Seder was relatively short because my father skipped a few pages, and it was not long before he would snap his Haggadah shut and say, "Serve supper, Sadie." Despite the brevity of the service, we knew what everything on the Seder plate meant.

The Seder plate is the same the world over, though recipes for the symbols may vary. A bitter herb, usually a bit of horseradish root, symbolizes the bitterness of slavery. Charoses, in our home a mixture of grated apple, sweet red wine, honey and cinnamon, recalls the mortar the Israelites were forced to plaster between bricks. A roasted lamb shank bone symbolizes the roasted lamb they ate the night before their deliverance. A roasted egg reminds us of on-going life, fresh parsley means spring and the salt water in which to dip it is a reminder of tears shed in slavery. Of most importance, however, is matzo, the unleavened bread eaten throughout Passover, which recalls the Israelites' haste to leave Egypt, without time to let their bread rise.

As my parents grew older, the Seders moved to our home and to our children's. (The three families take turns hosting the holidays.) With the moves have come changes. Along with the central Seder plate, we have individual Seder plates filled with the symbolic foods to avoid passing during the service.

Sometimes, there is a slip of paper tucked under the plate indicating a job, such as clearing, loading the dishwasher, pouring coffee. With this method, the meal that possibly uses more dishes and silver than any other is cleared and cleaned up easily.

And the list of guests grows. Since that Seder in 1943, we continue to record their names in Dad's Hagaddah. The inside cover and flyleaf are covered in his precise sculptural handwriting with names of family and friends, some I remember and some I do not. Mother pasted sheets of paper into the Hagaddah to accommodate the passing years, and often, she was the recorder in her loopy cheerful script. Then there is my handwriting, and now, that of our children.

The Story of Matzo

Matzo, the star of Passover, predates the Exodus from Egypt. After the harvest in ancient times, farmers destroyed the starter used to raise the bread and ate only unleavened bread made with flour from the new crop. Historians think they did it to express gratitude for a good crop of wheat, with hope for a good one the next year.

How, then, did the bread rise without a starter? Nature stepped in: a mixture of flour and water will attract air-borne yeast spores, which will leaven the bread. For this reason, flour for Passover matzo is closely guarded from harvest to baking to make sure it remains dry and unleavened.

Matzo Brei

Serves 4

We like our matzo brei seasoned with sugar and cinnamon, something like French Toast. But it's good with salt and freshly ground pepper, too.

1 cup milk
4 whole matzos
4 eggs
½ teaspoon kosher salt
2 tablespoons butter or extra virgin olive oil
¼ cup sugar mixed with 1 tablespoon cinnamon or kosher salt and freshly ground pepper to taste

1. Heat the milk to scalding (just below the boiling point).

2. Break the matzos into a 1-quart bowl. Pour the hot milk over them, cover and set aside to let the matzos absorb some of the milk.

3. When cool, mix in the eggs, one at a time. Stir in the salt.

4. Melt the butter in a skillet. Pour the matzo mixture into skillet and cook and stir it over medium heat until the brei is set. Remove the skillet from the heat before the brei gets too firm, because it will continue cooking off the heat.

5. Serve immediately with sugar and cinnamon or salt and pepper to taste.

Imps in the Kitchen

The late I.B. Singer, Jewish-Polish-American author, wrote often about life in the shtetls of Eastern Europe. A shtetl was a Jewish village with a rabbi, a baker, a butcher, a teacher, families and invisible imps who provoked all sorts of trouble. In Singer's stories, they lived mainly in the kitchen where they soured the milk, curdled the cream and kept the bread from rising. That world Singer described died when the inhabitants of the shtetls came to America. But with them came the imps. "Imps in America?" you say. "Surely those imps were Singer's imagination."

Don't believe it. They live in our kitchens, too. For no apparent reason, the brisket that made the cook famous comes out dry and stringy. Hard-boiled eggs develop green rings and the Jell-O does not set. Who but imps would have spoiled the food?

My mother was beset with imps. Her roast chicken was succulent and juicy with an aroma that made you hungry. Her Jell-O slipped out of the mold intact, with just a little pat from her, and her apple pie was the best in the world. But her matzo balls were hard as rocks. She would spend hours in the kitchen on the day of the Seder, making batch after batch of matzo balls, each heavier than the next. "Why can't I make matzo balls?" she would sigh.

I, on the other hand, who could never unmold Jell-O, who frequently serves chickens already roasted from the markets and rarely bake pies, do know how to make good matzo balls. Or so I thought. A few years ago, something happened. Instead of being light and fluffy, they came out hard with greenish centers. The longer I cooked them, the worse they got.

What could have happened? Should I not have covered them? Should I have simmered them? Boiled them? Did I cook them too long? Did I forget to salt the water? Did I uncover them while they cooked? Did I crowd the pot? Was the pot too big? Like Mother, I walked around my kitchen, sighing, "Why can't I make matzo balls?" Of course, now I know that imps have moved into my kitchen, surely the same ones that bedeviled my mother.

Matzo Balls

Makes about 24 1-inch matzo balls

I use oil in which onions have been sautéed instead of schmaltz (rendered chicken fat).

2 tablespoons extra virgin olive oil
¼ cup minced onion
2 eggs, separated
1 tablespoon finely minced fresh parsley
½ cup matzo meal
½ teaspoon kosher salt

1. Put the oil and onion in a sauté pan and cook slowly until the onion just begins to color. Set aside to cool.

2. Beat the egg whites until stiff. Set aside.

3. Stir the egg yolks. Stir in the cooled oil with the onions and the parsley.

4. Stir in the matzo meal and salt, a little at a time.

5. Stir in about one fourth of the beaten egg whites to lighten the mixture. Gently stir in the remaining whites, making sure there are no lumps of meal.

6. Cover and refrigerate about 2 hours or until the mixture is thick enough to form into balls. If necessary, refrigerate it longer.

7. Bring 3 quarts of salted water to a boil in a large pot. With wet hands, form the dough into 1-inch balls. They will expand with cooking.

8. Add all the balls to the boiling water. Simmer them covered about 45 minutes. Test for doneness. The interior of the matzo balls should be same color as the exterior.

9. Transfer the cooked matzo balls to warm chicken soup.

Note:
Never crowd the pot. If doubling the recipe, use 2 pots of water.

Savory Dumplings

Makes about 2 dozen

They make Spring Vegetable Soup a complete meal.

1 cup finely minced onion
1½ tablespoons extra virgin olive oil
1 garlic clove, minced
1 cup cooked chicken or beef
1 egg
⅓ cup matzo meal
2 tablespoons fresh parsley
1 teaspoon kosher salt
¼ teaspoon white pepper
2 cups chicken broth

1. Sauté the onion in the oil until it begins to soften, about 6 minutes. Add the garlic and sauté 2 minutes more. Set aside.

2. Mince the cooked chicken or beef. A food processor works well. Add the onions and garlic, the egg, matzo meal, parsley, salt and pepper and process for 30 seconds.

3. With wet hands, form 1-inch dumplings. Bring the broth to a simmer. Drop the dumplings into the broth and simmer covered about 20 minutes.

4. Lift the dumplings out of the broth with a slotted spoon and add them to Chicken or Spring Vegetable soup. Strain the broth they were cooked in and add it to the soup.

Note:
Another option is to stuff mushroom caps with the dumpling mixture. Preheat the oven to 400 degrees. Brush the insides of 12 large mushrooms caps with olive oil. Stuff the caps and bake them about 20 minutes in the upper level of the oven, until the mushrooms are tender when pierced with a small sharp knife.

A Rosh Hashanah Memory

My family was not especially observant. Mother never served pork, but shrimp were all right. She lit Sabbath candles, but we never went to Sabbath services. On Rosh Hashanah and Yom Kippur, we walked to Temple Beth Israel, the little synagogue on High Street, to attend services. My father would have skipped services entirely if Yom Kippur fell on a Saturday, the busiest day at his clothing store, but Mother wouldn't allow it.

Despite this, the congregation elected my father president. He was a good businessman, and they hoped he would pull Beth Israel out of debt, no small feat during World War II with a congregation of only fifty families.

The congregation was Orthodox in deference to the majority of Belleville's Jews. The men in yarmulkes and talaysim sat apart from the women in pretty hats and new fall suits. Rosh Hashanah was a social as well as a religious day, and at times, the chatter of the congregants overwhelmed the prayers from the bema. When the Rabbi could bear it no longer, someone would bang a prayer book on a bookstand and shout "Shah," and for a time, it was quiet.

People my age often sat outside on the front steps of the synagogue, listening to the World Series on someone's portable radio. But I always returned to my seat for my father's speech. As congregation president, his job was to wish everyone a happy New Year, welcome guests, announce the synagogue's financial status and read the names of Jewish men and women from Belleville in the service.

Dad always waited until Rosh Hashanah morning to compose his speech. During the services, he made notes on the flyleaf of a prayer book—a double sin by any standard. One man, who was usually on the bema with the Rabbi, tapped my father on the shoulder as he was writing. I was sure a reprimand was forthcoming, but all he said was "Joe, don't forget to mention my son. He's in Italy."

When services ended and when everyone had wished everyone a happy New Year, we walked home to a sumptuous lunch with freshly baked round challah and new honey, symbolic of the New Year. And despite an unorthodox president, the "shahs" and the World Series, the prayers in Temple Beth Israel were answered, because by the next Rosh Hashanah, the war was over and the synagogue was solvent.

First Place: *TableTalk* Challah Contest

Makes 5 (1-pound) loaves

Adapted from *Myrna Hershman's Challah,* the clear winner.

2 cups lukewarm water, 105 to 115 degrees
3 packages rapid rise yeast
1 cup sugar, divided
1 cup extra virgin olive oil
8 cups bread or unbleached flour, divided, plus more if necessary
1 teaspoon kosher salt
4 eggs
1 beaten egg for glazing
1 tablespoon each sugar, poppy or sesame seeds to garnish, optional

1. **Proofing the Yeast.** Mix the water and yeast in a 2-cup glass or pottery bowl. Add 1 teaspoon of the sugar. Stir with a fork and set aside in a draft-free place about 10 minutes or until the mixture starts to bubble. If the mixture does not bubble, your yeast is old or your water too hot or cold. Start over.

2. **Mixing the Dough.** Combine the yeast mixture in a large bowl with ¾ cup sugar, the oil and 3 cups flour. Stir until it looks like pancake batter. Cover the bowl lightly and set aside in a draft-free place for 30 minutes.

3. After the yeast mixture has rested for 30 minutes, beat the 4 eggs and add them to the bowl. Combine the remaining flour and sugar with the salt and add to the bowl. Stir well or work the dough with your hands. If it is sticky, flour your hands.

4. **Kneading the Dough.** Turn the dough onto a floured surface. Slap the dough down; fold it over from bottom to top. With the heels of your hands, push the dough away from you. Do a quarter turn with the dough. Repeat the process of folding and pushing the dough away from you with the heels of your hands and turning it for about 10 minutes, until the dough is smooth. Flour your hands if the dough is sticky.

5. **First Rising.** Place the dough in an oiled bowl, cover with a damp cloth and set aside in a draft-free place for 2 hours or until the dough has doubled in size. To know if it has raised enough, stick a finger in the dough. If an indentation remains, the dough is ready to be shaped into loaves. If not, let it rest a little longer.

6. **Shaping the Dough.** Pull the batter away from the sides of the bowl and knead it lightly. Divide it into 5 portions. Work with one portion at a time, keeping the rest covered.

7. Divide each portion into 4 pieces. Roll 3 of them into long ropes of equal length; braid them, tucking ends under. Divide the last piece into 3 ropes, which will be short. Braid them and place the braid on top of the loaf. Place the loaf on a lightly greased baking sheet. Continue with the remaining portions.

8. **Second Rising.** Cover the loaves lightly and let them rise for 30 minutes in a draft-free place. Preheat the oven to 350 degrees.

9. **Baking the Challah.** Brush the tops of the loaves with the beaten egg. Sprinkle with sugar, poppy or sesame seeds and bake 25-35 minutes or until bottoms are firm. Because rising takes place in the oven in the first 15 minutes, do not open the oven door.

10. The bread is done when it sounds hollow when thumped on the bottom.

Some notes:

1. I often add a cup of raisins in step 3.

2. You can make fewer larger loaves and simply braid them. For round challah, roll the dough into a 12-inch rope. Starting in the center, coil the dough into a circle, tucking the end under.

3. To start challah the day before, do steps 1-5, refrigerating the bowl of dough covered with a damp cloth. Punch it down before you go to bed—it could climb out of the bowl. The next day, let the dough come to room temperature, about 1 hour. Punch it down and divide it into portions. Let it rest about 10 minutes. Shape it and let it rise about 55 minutes. Bake as above.

My Grandmother

My grandparents, Paulina and Isaac Peskind, moved from St. Louis to Belleville in 1904, where they opened a clothing store on Main Street. But business was not good, and peddling, which would have helped sales, was forbidden in Belleville. My grandmother, (not my grandfather!) met with Mayor Kern, to ask if my grandfather might sell merchandise from a horse-driven wagon. She must have been highly persuasive because he gave his permission, which indeed helped business and enabled them to move the store to a better block of Main Street.

(Many years later, my father heard the story of his mother's request from his friend, a later Mayor Kern, who had heard it from his father.)

When Grandma was not working in the store, she cooked for her family of eight, though at times there were more—when a sister had a new baby, grandma took the two-year-old home with her until her sister regained her strength. She baked bread every day and put up hundreds of quarts of strawberry preserves.

After their sons took over the store, she and Grandpa moved to St. Louis and when Grandpa died, my grandmother lived with her daughter, my Aunt Rose and Uncle Max. But for a few months of the year, she visited her other children.

We loved when she came to our house. Mother made dresses for her out of the lavender prints my grandmother favored, and Grandma baked challah and pletzel, a heavenly golden flat bread topped with diced onions. We ate it hot from the oven.

Grandma survived Aunt Rose's death and later that of one of her sons with enormous courage. In her later years, she refused to live with any of her remaining children and moved instead into the Jewish Center for the Aged. She asked my father to bring her women's hosiery from the store, which she sold to nursing home attendants at three pairs for a dollar, a bargain even in those days. The proceeds, or, as my father was fond of saying, her "profits," she divided among those old men at the Center whom she knew had no money. "A man has to have a little money in his pockets," she would say.

My grandmother lived into her late nineties. On one of my visits, I asked her about coming to America. She told me her father died right before the journey from Europe, and her mother came alone with two little girls. "My mother remarried as soon as we got here," Grandma said. "It was not so good, Honey, but what's a woman to do alone in a new country?"

I regret that I know nothing of her parents or what life was like in Europe or what my father was like as a child. And I regret not having her pletzel recipe.

First Place: *TableTalk* Kugel Contest

Serves 10-12

Adapted from *Albert Glassman's Pineapple Kugel Supreme*. It has become a family favorite.

6 eggs, beaten
1 cup brown sugar
½ teaspoon kosher salt
½ teaspoon pepper
1 (20-ounce) can pineapple tidbits
½ cup raisins
1 pound medium noodles

Topping
1 cup cornflake crumbs crushed from 2 cups cornflakes, or other cereal crumbs
1 cup brown sugar
8 tablespoons (1 stick) pareve • margarine, melted or ½ cup extra virgin olive oil

1. Preheat the oven to 350 degrees. Grease a 9x13-inch baking dish.

2. Combine the eggs with brown sugar, salt, pepper, pineapple with juice and raisins.

3. Cook the noodles according to package directions. Drain them and when slightly cool, stir them into the eggs.

4. Pour the kugel into the prepared pan.

5. For the topping, combine the crumbs and brown sugar with the margarine. Sprinkle on top of the kugel. Bake at once or refrigerate to bake later. Bring to room temperature 1 hour before baking.

6. Bake 1 to 1½ hours or until the kugel is brown and firm. If too brown before becoming firm, cover it loosely with foil.

• Pareve foods contain neither meat nor dairy products and can be served at a meat or dairy meal. Pareve foods are labeled.

Kreplach: Not for the Timid

Mother told this story every time she made kreplach.

There once was a little boy named Sammy who was afraid of kreplach. Whenever he saw a bowl of chicken soup with kreplach he would scream with fright:

Ahhh! Kreplach!

His poor mother was so upset, she went to a child psychologist who told her to have Sammy watch her make kreplach, step by step, so he wouldn't be afraid.

The next day, she had Sammy sit at the kitchen table.

See, Sammy, I am measuring flour into a bowl. You're not afraid, are you Sammy?

No, Mama.

She broke the eggs into the bowl. She added some salt and a little water.

You're not afraid, are you, Sammy?

No, Mama.

She mixed the dough; she kneaded it; she rolled it thin. She cut it into small squares, and in the middle of each square, she put some meat and fried onions.

You're not afraid, are you, Sammy?

No, Mama.

Then she folded the dough over the meat into triangles, pressed the edges together and put them in a pot of boiling water.

You're not afraid, are you, Sammy?

No, Mama.

Soon, the kreplach floated to the top of the pot. With a slotted spoon, she lifted two kreplach out of the pot into a bowl and covered them with chicken soup. She placed it in front of Sammy.

Sammy looked down at the bowl and screamed with fright:

Ahhh! Kreplach!

Like Sammy, I've had to overcome my own fear of kreplach because my previous attempts fell apart in boiling water. Now, when I make them, I use Mother's filling with dough that can be rolled paper-thin, and they hold together when I boil them.

Kreplach

Makes about 3 dozen

Filling
¾ pound cooked pot roast or brisket, ground or 1 pound uncooked ground beef
1 small onion, finely minced
1 garlic clove, finely minced
1 tablespoon of extra virgin olive oil
1 egg, lightly beaten
Kosher salt and freshly ground pepper to taste

1. Sauté the cooked meat, onion and garlic in the oil on medium heat about 8 minutes, until the onion and garlic are softened and beginning to brown. Set aside to cool.

2. If using uncooked meat, sauté it in the oil for 5 minutes. Add the onion and garlic and continue until they are softened and beginning to brown. Set aside to cool.

3. Stir in the egg, salt and pepper. Set aside or refrigerate to use later.

Dough
3 cups flour plus a bit more
¾ teaspoon kosher salt
3 eggs
About 3-5 tablespoons water

1. Combine the flour and salt in a food processor fitted with a steel blade. Pulse a few times. Add the eggs and pulse a few times until the dough is crumbly.

2. With the machine running, add some of the water through the tube, using just enough so that the dough forms a ball. Too much water makes the dough sticky.

3. Add a bit more flour and process about 30 seconds more to knead the dough. It should be very smooth.

4. Wrap the dough well in plastic wrap so it does not dry out; let it rest at room temperature for 30 minutes.

5. Divide the dough into 3 portions. Work with 1 portion of dough at a time, keeping the rest well wrapped. Roll the dough to a rectangle about 9- by 12- inches.

6. Cut into 12 (3-inch) squares. Put a heaping teaspoon of filling on each square. Dab water along two sides. Fold the dough to form a triangle. Press the edges together with the tines of a fork. At this point, you can freeze the kreplach to cook later.

7. To cook, drop 12 of the kreplach into large pot of lightly salted boiling water and simmer about 8 minutes. Remove them from the water with a slotted spoon.

8. Cook the remaining kreplach. Refrigerate them covered.

9. To serve, reheat them in hot chicken soup.

Notes:
1. Always prepare the filling first.
2. The amount of dough and the amount of filling never come out even.

Main Dishes

Black Circle Series, detail
Waterless Lithography. 10" x 10".

Peace in the Middle East

When Billy and I toured Egypt in 1981, it was peaceful in the Middle East. Anwar Sadat, the president of Egypt (president for life, Maya, our Egyptian guide called him) and Menachem Begin, prime minister of Israel, had shared the Nobel Peace Price in 1978. Israeli tourists were visiting Egypt, though the reverse was not true, and Israeli purveyors were selling meat to Cairo hotels.

But soldiers lined the streets of Cairo with guns at their sides. Guards at the doors of the Nile Hilton Hotel checked our parcels and purses, and one who knew a smattering of English asked jokingly if I had a bomb in my purse.

Despite the soldiers, we toured Egypt. It was like living within the History Channel—Cairo, the Pyramids, the Sphinx, Luxor, Abu Simbel, the souks. We found it all fascinating. And we liked the food, much like what we ate later in Israel, but then, of course, they share the Mediterranean breadbasket.

Included on our tour was a cocktail party in an apartment building on an island in the Nile where we met Leila and Napo. Leila was Egyptian and Napo, the El Al agent in Cairo, was German. When we told them we were interested in Egyptian food, they invited us to visit them.

Napo picked us up at the Nile Hilton and drove us through Cairo's heavy traffic to their apartment in the Zamalek district of Cairo, once called the garden district of the city. The elevator to their apartment, in what had been a handsome building, rose only to the 14th floor, and we walked up to the 15th. No one had gotten around to fixing the elevator, Napo told us.

Leila had prepared tea, including baklava and konafa, pastries rich with honey and nuts, which she had purchased. She told us about Bamia Stew, an okra dish dating back to the Pharaohs, and Chakchouka, a supper or luncheon dish of bell peppers, tomatoes, onions and eggs popular in Egypt.

After tea, while Napo and Billy smoked cigars, Leila asked me about food in America. When we returned home, we sent her a copy of *Joy of Cooking* by Irma Rombauer and Napo, a box of good cigars.

A few months after our tour, Anwar Sadat was assassinated and the regime changed in Egypt, and we had not yet heard if Leila and Napo had received our box. At last, they wrote from West Germany that they were sorry it had taken them so long to thank us for the book and cigars, but they had left Egypt in a hurry. I replied to the West German address, but we never heard from them again.

Chakchouka

Serves 4-6

Chakchouka is a colorful and spicy Tunisian vegetable and egg dish that is served throughout the Middle East. It good for breakfast, brunch or lunch.

2 bell peppers, green, red or yellow, seeded and sliced into strips
2 onions, thinly sliced
4 tablespoons butter or extra virgin olive oil
8 small fresh tomatoes or canned ones of good quality, halved
Kosher salt and freshly ground pepper to taste
6 eggs

1. Sauté the peppers and onions in the butter or oil in a large skillet. Let the mixture stew gently for a few minutes.

2. When the peppers are soft, add the tomatoes and cook several minutes longer, until the tomatoes are soft. Season to taste with salt and pepper.

3. Break the eggs into the pan, arranging them in sections for serving. Or, for a creamy texture, stir the eggs into the vegetables. Cover the pan and cook a few minutes more, until the egg whites are set.

4. Slip the Chakchouka onto a serving plate and cut as for a pie, or serve at table from the skillet.

5. Variations: Add browned ground meat or diced boiled potatoes to the vegetables before adding the eggs.

A Memorable Meal in Stresa

It was not fancy in any way. In fact, it could not have been plainer. But this meal in Stresa was one Billy and I remember with enormous pleasure.

We were touring the Lake Country of northern Italy before going on to Venice to cooking demonstrations by Marcella Hazan. We had just gotten off a boat, which had taken us to the islands in *Lago Maggiore*, and we were wandering the streets of Stresa, looking for a place to have lunch. It was an overcast cool day in late October. Nothing appeared open, until we looked through a dark bar opening on to a sunny back yard filled with tables and diners. Truly, it appeared to be the only sunshine in Stresa, and we gratefully took a table.

We puzzled our way through the menu with our meager knowledge of Italian. We glanced at the table next to us. The couple was having sautéed trout, boiled potatoes dressed in butter, good bread and a bottle of white wine.

We told the waitress we would have what our neighbors were having. "Good choice," she said in good English. "It's a salmon trout freshly caught from Lago Maggiore."

The trout arrived, crisp on the outside and deep pink inside, thus its name. It had been sautéed in olive oil with fresh sage leaves that were crisp and nutty. The potatoes and bread were good and the cold white wine completed our memorable meal.

Trout Sautéed with Fresh Sage

Serves 4

If you are not near *Lago Maggiore*, any good lake trout will do.

4 trout filets, about ½ pound each
¼ cup flour
Kosher salt and freshly ground pepper to taste
3 tablespoons extra virgin olive oil or more if needed
8 fresh sage leaves

1. Wash the fish in cold water and pat it dry with paper towels.

2. Combine the flour with the seasonings on a large piece of waxed paper.

3. In a large skillet that will hold the fish without crowding, heat the oil over medium heat.

4. When the oil is hot, dust the fish with the seasoned flour, shaking off any excess. Add the sage to the pan. Sauté the filets on one side until a light crust has formed. Turn and sauté the other side. Serve at once, with the crisp sage leaves, which develop a nutty taste with sautéing.

The Early Bird Special

Birds we never see in Missouri, except in the birdhouse of the zoo, fly freely here on Longboat Key, Florida. Gulls wing their way across the golf course outside our window, like a length of white lace against the green; herons and egrets, red beaked ibis and roseate spoonbills peck the grasses; ducks sail in formation on the shallow ponds, disappearing into the water to feed, while turkey vultures soar overhead checking the landscape for carrion. All are eating.

But a walk on the beach late morning or late afternoon is where you see the real eating. (Perhaps this is where the "early bird special" got its name.) First to arrive are the pelicans, riding the air currents with wingspans close to seven feet. When we see them bobbing on the Gulf of Mexico, we think the waters are healthy, that there is no Red Tide to kill the small fish they feed on. They reconnoiter the waves, flying high, until they spot their prey and then, with enormous speed, dive into the water for the catch. Usually, a few gulls hover nearby. Perhaps they know the pelicans know where the fish are. (One day, we saw a gull perched on the head of a pelican for a better view.) Sandpipers flit about the beach, digging out tiny sea creatures with their sharp beaks.

Rarely do we see ospreys, but one afternoon, we saw one perched on a branch of a tree outside our window. His breast was snow white and the rest of him, a rich brown. (Male coloring, our bird book said.) He perched there, eating a large fish with pinkish flesh. We watched him for over two hours, and he was still eating when the sun went down. After that, we could no longer see him, and by morning, he had flown away.

Ginger Sesame Salmon

Serve 4

It's good hot, at room temperature or cold.

4 salmon filets, about 6 ounces each, boned •
1½ cups dry white wine
4 lemon slices
½ cup diced celery
Sprigs of fresh dill or parsley or both
1 garlic clove, minced
1 tablespoon sesame oil
2 teaspoons soy sauce
2 teaspoons rice vinegar
1 tablespoon peeled and minced fresh ginger
2 scallions diced, including crisp green parts
Lemon slices, to garnish

1. Preheat the oven to 375 degrees. Place the filets skin side down in shallow baking pan. Pour the wine over the filets and top them with lemon slices, celery, dill and parsley.

2. Cover the pan with foil and bake about 30 minutes or until the filets are opaque. Remove from oven and keep covered until serving. The fish can be refrigerated at this point if you wish to serve it cold.

3. Sauté the garlic in sesame oil until it starts to brown. Watch carefully so that it does not burn. Set it aside.

4. Combine the soy sauce with vinegar and ginger and set it aside.

5. To serve, remove the filets from the cooking liquid, discarding lemon, celery and herbs. Place the filets on a platter or on individual plates.

6. Pour on the soy sauce mixture. Sprinkle with green onions and drizzle the garlic and oil on top. Serve with fresh lemon slices.

• Use tweezers to remove any stray bones.

Glazed Salmon Filets

Serves 4

3 tablespoons soy sauce
3 tablespoons sugar or mirin (sweet Japanese rice wine)
1½ teaspoons peeled grated fresh ginger
4 (7-8) ounce salmon filets, boned •

1. Combine the soy sauce and sugar in a small saucepan. Cook over low heat stirring constantly. When sugar is dissolved, add the ginger and simmer 3 minutes more. Cool and refrigerate up to a week.

2. Line a baking pan with foil or use a disposable pan. Put the salmon in the pan skin side down and brush on the glaze. Broil the salmon 4 inches from the heat for 10 minutes. Do not turn it. Serve hot or at room temperature with additional glaze.

3. Do not keep the fish at room temperature more than 1 hour. If necessary, refrigerate it until 1 hour before serving.

• Use tweezers to remove any stray bones.

Salmon Cakes with Cilantro Lime Cream

Serves 2

These make a wonderful quick lunch or supper, especially if you have leftover salmon. But they are good with canned salmon, too.

Salmon Cakes
6-7 ounces cooked or canned salmon
1 egg, beaten
3 tablespoons dry unflavored breadcrumbs
4 tablespoons chopped fresh chives
2 tablespoons chopped shallots
2 tablespoons mayonnaise
2 teaspoons fresh lime juice
2 teaspoons chopped cilantro
Kosher salt and freshly ground pepper to taste
1 tablespoon extra virgin olive oil

Cilantro Lime Cream
¼ cup sour cream
2 teaspoons chopped cilantro
2 tablespoons fresh lime juice
Kosher salt and freshly ground pepper to taste

1. Flake the salmon with a fork. If using canned salmon, drain it and mash the bones into the salmon. Stir in the egg, breadcrumbs, chives, shallots, mayonnaise, lime juice, cilantro, salt and pepper. Form into 2 cakes.

2. Coat a sauté pan with the oil. Sauté the cakes in a medium hot pan about 3 minutes on each side or until golden brown.

3. Combine the ingredients of the Cilantro Lime Cream. Garnish the cakes with the Cilantro Lime Cream and sprigs of fresh cilantro.

Leftovers

When my parents, Sadie and Joe Peskind, married in 1923, they knew little about each other. They simply met, fell in love, married and lived together for over fifty years.

But they had much in common, which may have made up for not knowing each other well. Both were children of first generation Jewish Americans with similar values and economic backgrounds, and both had been reared in small towns. They knew before the wedding that my father would be at his store and my mother, at home, rearing the children and keeping house.

Every evening, Dad came home from the store before six, and dinner was served promptly at six. But one night, shortly after the honeymoon, they had their first quarrel. Dad sat down to dinner, looked at his plate and said, "Sadie, what's this?"

"Why, Joe," she said. "It is the rest of last night's chicken."

"You mean it's leftover?" he asked. "Of course," she said.

He put down his fork, refolded his napkin and announced, "I don't eat leftovers."

Without a word, Mother picked up their plates, walked to the garbage can and disposed of their dinners. "If you won't eat leftovers, I won't eat leftovers," she said.

Actually, she loved leftovers. She had grown up eating them every night for supper. Dinner in Forrest City, Arkansas was at noon, and her father came home from his clothing store to a full meal of soup, meat or chicken, potatoes, vegetables and pie. Supper was leftovers. Grandma would make fresh biscuits to go with the fried chicken and applesauce that had been dinner.

My father, on the other hand, had never been exposed to leftovers. In Belleville, dinner was the evening meal, much like the southern dinner served at noon. With six children plus my grandparents, everything my grandmother put on the table was eaten.

And not only at dinner. For an after-school snack, my grandmother placed a loaf of homemade bread and a jar of her strawberry preserves on the kitchen table. The six children did not stop eating until the preserves jar was empty and the bread gone.

My father never learned to like leftovers, unless they were chicken, his favorite food. Mother would dispense the remainder of last night's dinner for lunch for the children and herself. I still love leftovers.

Chicken Roasted with Sage

Serves 4

This succulent chicken dish can be made the day before and reheated successfully. It works equally well with turkey legs and thighs.

1 (3-pound) chicken cut into 8 pieces or any combination of pieces
¼ cup flour
2 tablespoons vegetable oil
Kosher salt and freshly ground pepper to taste
2 tablespoons extra virgin olive oil
2 cups sliced onions
1 tablespoon minced fresh garlic
16 fresh sage leaves, bundled with kitchen twine
½ cup dry white wine or dry Marsala wine
2 teaspoons tomato paste
½ cup chicken broth, homemade or canned
3 tablespoons minced fresh parsley

1. Preheat the oven to 350 degrees. Rinse the chicken under cold running water and pat it dry with paper towels.

2. Put the vegetable oil into a heavy skillet. Turn the heat to medium high.

3. Dust the chicken with the flour. Shake off any excess flour. Add the chicken to the pan but do not crowd it. Sauté the chicken until it is crusty on both sides and starting to brown. Set the browned pieces aside on a plate and season them to taste with salt and pepper. Continue with the remaining pieces.

4. Pour off any fat left in the skillet and wipe it out with paper towels. Add the olive oil to the pan and stir in the onions. Sauté them about 10 minutes, until they are soft and translucent. Stir in the garlic and sage bundle and sauté about 5 minutes more. Add the wine.

5. Cook on high, scraping up any brown bits with a wooden spoon. Stir in the tomato paste and broth. Return the chicken to the pan. Cover it and bake about 1 hour, or until the chicken is tender. Turn off the oven.

6. If the chicken is not as brown as you wish, leave it in the oven uncovered for 10 minutes.

7. Lift the chicken out of the gravy; discard the sage bundle and strain the gravy, mashing the onions through the strainer. Combine the gravy and chicken. Sprinkle with the parsley and serve.

8. If not serving immediately, refrigerate the chicken and gravy separately and when cool, remove any fat from the top. To serve, combine the gravy and chicken and reheat it gently on medium heat or in a 350 oven for 20 minutes. Sprinkle with parsley and serve.

Note 1:
Boneless skinless thighs make a nice presentation. Before cooking, roll them to look like thighs with bones. Secure the edges with toothpicks. Proceed with the recipe but be sure to remove the toothpicks before serving.

Note 2:
For convenience, buy tomato paste in a tube.

Brunswick Stew

Serves 8

While researching southern cooking, I found this recipe for a wonderful make-ahead meal. Back in Virginia in the 1800's, squirrel was the main ingredient. We prefer chicken.

16 pieces of chicken
½ cup vegetable oil plus more as needed
½ cup flour plus more as needed
Kosher salt and freshly ground pepper to taste
3 tablespoons extra virgin olive oil
6 onions, thinly sliced
3 cups chicken stock or enough to barely cover chicken
6 tomatoes peeled and sliced or 1(14.5 ounce) can whole tomatoes, drained and sliced. (Reserve liquid for another use.)
3 red bell peppers, seeded and diced
½ teaspoon dried thyme

4 cups lima beans or green soybeans, frozen or fresh
4 cups okra, frozen or fresh
4 ears of fresh good-tasting corn
4 tablespoons chopped fresh parsley, to garnish

1. Preheat the oven to 350 degrees. Wash the chicken and pat it dry with white paper towels.

2. Put the vegetable oil in a heavy pan over medium heat. Dredge only a few pieces of the chicken with the flour, shaking off excess. Brown the chicken on both sides. Don't crowd the pan—the chicken will not brown. Set the browned pieces aside on a plate and season them to taste with salt and pepper.

3. Continue with the remaining chicken, adding more vegetable oil as needed.

4. When all the chicken has been browned, discard any remaining oil and wipe out the pan with paper towels. Add the olive oil to the pan, stir in the onions and cook on medium heat until they start to brown.

5. Return the chicken to the pan. Add the stock, tomatoes, peppers and thyme. Cover the pan and bake about 1 hour or until the chicken is tender. At this point, you may cool the stew and refrigerate it to be completed later or the next day.

6. To finish the stew, bring it to a simmer. Add the lima beans and okra, and simmer until the vegetables are tender, about 15 minutes.

7. Remove the kernels from a cob by holding a cob on end over a clean towel. With a sharp knife, strip off the kernels from the middle of the cob down. Reverse the cob and strip off the rest of the kernels. By doing half a cob at a time, the kernels do not scatter as far. Add to the stew and simmer 2 minutes.

8. Serve stew in large soup plates, because it will be like rich soup. Garnish with parsley. Offer good bread to sop up the sauce.

Classic Broiled Chicken

Chicken breasts, legs or thighs with skin and bones
Kosher salt and freshly ground pepper to taste

1. Place the rack in the oven about 4 inches from the flame or coils. Preheat the broiler to 450 degrees.

2. Season the pieces and place them on the broiler pan skin side down. Broil breasts 15 minutes and turn them for another 15. Broil legs and thighs 20 minutes and turn them for another 20. Serve at once.

Chicken Breasts Poached in the Microwave

4 boned and skinned chicken breasts, fresh or frozen
2 cups hot water
1 carrot, scrubbed
1 onion, unpeeled and halved
1 garlic clove, unpeeled and halved
2 tablespoons celery leaves
4 peppercorns
¼ teaspoon thyme

1. Put everything in a large microwave dish. Cover and microwave on high power about 18 minutes or until the chicken is tender. Frozen chicken will take lightly longer.

2. Cool the chicken in the stock. Use it for salad or sandwiches, or freeze it.

3. Strain the stock and freeze it to use later.

Chicken Gumbo

Serves 6

3 pounds chicken parts
1 pound chicken Andouille sausage
3 tablespoons extra virgin olive oil
1 pound okra, thickly sliced
1 large green bell pepper, coarsely chopped
1 large onion, coarsely chopped
2 celery ribs, coarsely chopped
4 garlic cloves, minced
1 (28-ounce) can of tomatoes with juice
2 teaspoons cumin
1 bay leaf
Kosher salt and freshly ground pepper to taste
4-5 teaspoons gumbo filé
12 tablespoons rice
2 tablespoons chopped scallions

1. Put the chicken and sausage in a pot, cover with water and cook until the chicken is tender, about 1 hour. When cool, discard the bones and skin from the chicken. Set the chicken and sausage aside. Reserve the stock, adding water if necessary to make 6 cups.

2. Add the oil to a large heavy pan. Add the okra and sauté until slightly soft, about 15 minutes.

3. Add the pepper, onion, celery, and garlic. Stir and cook another 10 minutes.

4. Add the reserved stock, the tomatoes, cumin, bay leaf, salt and pepper. Simmer uncovered 30 minutes.

5. Stir in the gumbo filé and the rice. Cook covered until the rice is tender.

6. Taste to correct seasonings with more salt, pepper and gumbo filé.

7. Before serving, cut the chicken into strips and slice the sausage. Add them to the gumbo and cook about 3 minutes. Garnish with scallions.

Thanksgiving Is Not a Jewish Holiday

Of course, Thanksgiving is not a Jewish holiday, though I once heard a young child declare it to be one. And why not? It commemorates the exodus of the Pilgrims from England to Massachusetts in their search for religious freedom, their survival of the sea crossing and living through the first winter.

Thanksgiving has what makes Jewish holidays so special: a reason to thank God, a reason to celebrate and a reason to dine on symbolic foods.

Furthermore, it is the meal at which everyone dines together, another likeness to a Jewish holiday. Often, guests contribute something to the feast, as the Indians did at the first Thanksgiving. We have them to thank for our tradition of roast turkey.

Many years ago, friends of our children brought sweet potatoes to our table, and now, they are ours. Our stuffing is another story, and from a story. While researching an article on foods in fiction, I reread Charles Dickens's *A Christmas Carol*. Dickens always provided his readers with a good meal. There at the Cratchit's Christmas dinner next to the largest turkey Ebenezer Scrooge could find was sage and onion stuffing, a typical English dish. I found a recipe for it in an English cookbook: bread, onions, ground pork and cream. Don't tell the English, but I converted it to bread, onions, ground turkey and chicken broth. It is a winner,

Not everyone has turkey for Thanksgiving, however. Too mundane, some say, preferring roast beef or roast duck. And sometimes, there are dishes considered unusual by mainstream Americans. Shortly before Thanksgiving a few years ago, I was picking up clothes at a tailor shop owned by a Vietnamese family. "And what are you having for Thursday's dinner?" I asked, making idle conversation. "Egg roll," the owner replied.

Another time, when visiting a grandchild's class before Thanksgiving, the teacher asked the children what their families were having for the great feast. "Chitlings," said a small African American child. The teacher wrote it on the blackboard next to stuffing, turkey and cranberries.

Why not egg roll or chitlings? What does it matter if Americans of diverse backgrounds celebrate the first great migration to America with their own traditions? Maybe that is what makes Thanksgiving so special.

Jim's Turkey

This method of roasting turkey has been around for a while, but we call it The Jim Firestone Turkey. He prepared it for his family on the day of his graduation from medical school. Even though he roasted it with the packet of giblets, intact, inside the bird, it was wonderful, and he was delighted with it.

1. Preheat the oven to 450 degrees. Line a shallow pan with 2 long pieces of heavy-duty foil, forming a cross. Place the turkey in the center.

2. Put ¼ of a small onion inside the turkey with a little seasoning of your choice and a few ribs of celery. Season the outside with kosher salt, pepper, garlic powder and mixed seasonings. Scatter diced onion around the turkey. Add no fat.

3. Close the foil over the turkey, leaving an air space between the breast and foil. Open the foil the last 25 minutes for browning.

4. Timetable for roasting:

6 lbs.	2 hours
8 lbs.	2 hours 20 minutes
10 lbs.	2 hours 45 minutes
12 lbs.	2 hours 55 minutes
14 lbs.	3 hours
20 lbs.	3 hours 30 minutes
22 lbs.	3 hours 45 minutes
24 lbs.	4 hours

Note: Allow 1 pound of turkey per serving.

Turkey Gravy

Makes about 4 cups

It's best to prepare the gravy base the day before cooking the turkey.

4 tablespoons vegetable oil
Turkey neck, gizzard and heart, chopped into pieces, wiped clean and dried
1 cup chopped onions
1 cup chopped carrots
1 cup dry white wine
2 cups chicken broth, homemade or canned
Kosher salt to taste
1 bay leaf
½ teaspoon thyme or sage

1. Heat the oil in a heavy saucepan. Add the neck, gizzard and heart and brown them well on all sides. Remove them from the pan.

2. Stir in the vegetables. Cover the pan and cook slowly about 8 minutes, until the vegetables are almost tender. Uncover the pan, raise the heat and brown them lightly.

3. Return the giblets to the pan; add the wine, broth and water as needed to cover the ingredients. Add 1 teaspoon salt, the bay leaf and thyme. Simmer partly covered for 2½ to 3 hours. Strain and refrigerate the stock. The next day, lift off any fat.

4. When the turkey is done, put it on a platter and let it rest 30 minutes before carving so that the juices can go back into the tissues.

5. Spoon the excess fat out of the roasting pan. Pour in the prepared stock. Put the roaster over a burner and stir over moderately high heat for several minutes, scraping the bottom of the pan with a wooden spoon. Taste to adjust seasonings.

6. Strain the gravy into a saucepan and spoon off the fat or lay a paper towel over the gravy and pick it up, taking the fat with it. If you want thicker gravy, combine ¼ cup cornstarch with ½ cup cold water. Stir into the gravy until it is thickened.

Sage And Onion Casserole

Serves 4-6

I came across this recipe in an English cookbook when researching food in Charles Dickens's novels. Sage and Onion Stuffing was on the menu at the Cratchit home in _A Christmas Carol_. I have replaced the ground pork with ground turkey and the milk with chicken broth, and I bake it in a casserole, not in the turkey. It's superb, but please, use fresh sage. The dried in the jar won't be the same. While it is usually a Thanksgiving side dish, it can be a main dish.

½ pound ground raw turkey breast
2 tablespoons extra virgin olive oil, divided
1 pound yellow onions, finely chopped
1 egg
1 cup chicken broth
10 fresh sage leaves finely chopped (about 1 tablespoon)
2 cups fresh whole wheat or white coarse breadcrumbs made from dense bread
1 teaspoon kosher salt
½ teaspoon freshly ground pepper
6 tablespoons slivered almonds, divided

1. Preheat the oven to 350 degrees. Grease a 1½-quart baking dish.

2. Sauté the turkey in 1 tablespoon oil. When it has lost its raw look and is starting to brown, remove it from the pan and set aside.

3. Add the remaining oil to same pan and sauté the onions until they are soft.

4. In a large bowl, beat the egg. Add the meat, onions, broth, sage, breadcrumbs, salt, pepper and ¼ cup almonds.

5. Put the mixture in the prepared baking dish and sprinkle with the remaining almonds. Bake 40 minutes or until it starts to brown.

Note:
To insure a well-seasoned stuffing before baking it, sauté a tablespoon or so in a skillet. Taste and add salt, pepper or more chopped sage leaves, as necassary.

The Plate Lunch

I was eight years old the first time I ate alone in a restaurant. Because my grade school had no cafeteria, only a lunchroom we shared with the janitor on rainy days when we brought lunch from home, I usually walked home for lunch. But that day, the day I ate out alone, Mother was unexpectedly not going to be at home, so she called the school to tell them to tell me to buy lunch at the Green Tea Pot, a small restaurant across the street from school. She said she would stop by later to pay the bill.

I was thrilled. It was to be my first chance to eat in a restaurant alone with no parents and no older sister, who was by then in junior high school. Lunchtime came. I sat down at a booth in the Green Tea Pot, feeling older than my eight years. May, the waitress, asked me what I wanted.

"I want a hamburger, a bowl of chili and the plate lunch."

"You want what?"

I said it again. "I want a hamburger, a bowl of chili and the plate lunch.'"

The owner, Mr. Dunk came back to my booth. He leaned over me, both hands gripping the table. "You say you want a hamburger, bowl of chili and the plate lunch?"

"Yes, please."

"Do you know what a plate lunch is?"

"Yes."

I lied. I had never before seen a plate lunch. Mr. Dunk walked away. May returned, carrying a tray bearing a hamburger, a bowl of chili and a thick white china plate divided into three sections filled with meatloaf, mashed potatoes with gravy and peas.

Now I knew what a plate lunch was.

First I ate the chili and the hamburger, recalling too late that was what my sister always ordered for us. Then, I started on the plate lunch. Slowly, I ate the whole thing. Occasionally, May drifted by to see how I was doing. So did Mr. Dunk.

By a quarter of one, all the dishes in front of me were empty, and I walked slowly back to school. Mr. Dunk and May must have marveled at my appetite. So did Mother when she paid the bill.

Hamburgers with Browned Onions

Serves 4

There are a million ways to make hamburgers. My mother's hamburgers we lovingly called "bread burgers" because she put so much bread into them. They were good, nonetheless, because she used plenty of onion. We use onion, too, but save the bread for the bun.

2 tablespoons extra virgin olive oil
2 large onions, peeled and sliced into rounds about ½-inch thick
1 pound ground sirloin
1 tablespoon soy sauce
1 tablespoon water
1 teaspoon kosher salt

1. Preheat the oven to 200 degrees. Put the oil in a sauté pan large enough to hold the onions in one layer.

2. Turn the heat to medium and add the onions. Sauté them, turning frequently, until they brown on both sides. Set them in the oven to stay warm.

3. Combine the meat with the soy sauce and water. Form into 4 patties.

4. Sprinkle the salt in the bottom of another sauté pan, preferably cast iron. Turn the heat to medium-high, and when drops of water "dance" in the skillet, add the hamburgers.

5. Adjust the heat to brown the hamburgers but not burn them. Turn them once or twice until they are done the way you want them. I always use one hamburger (mine) as a tester.

6. Serve at once on toasted buns with browned onions.

My Chili

Makes about 10 cups

It's healthy and full of flavor—a good main dish for lunch or supper. It's vegetarian if made with mushrooms.

3 tablespoons extra virgin olive oil, divided
1 pound ground beef, ground turkey breast or chopped shitake mushroom caps
1 cup chopped onion
2 garlic cloves, minced
1 cup dry Marsala wine or water
1 (28-ounce) can of tomatoes, puréed if whole
1 red bell pepper, seeded and diced, optional
2-3 tablespoons brown sugar or to taste
2-4 tablespoons chili powder or to taste
1-3 teaspoons ground cumin or to taste
¼ teaspoon ground red pepper
Kosher salt and freshly ground pepper, to taste
2 (15-ounce) cans kidney beans, rinsed and drained
1 (10-ounce) package frozen corn, optional

1. Put 2 tablespoons oil in a heavy pan, turn the heat to medium and sauté the meat until it loses its raw look and starts to brown. (Do the same if using mushrooms.) With a slotted spoon, remove the meat or mushrooms from the pan and set aside.

2. Add the remaining oil and onion to the pan and sauté until the onion is translucent, about 8 minutes. Add garlic and sauté 2 minutes more. Pour in the wine, turn up the heat and cook until almost all the wine has evaporated.

3. Return the meat or mushrooms to the pan; add the tomatoes with their juice, optional red pepper, brown sugar, chili powder, ground cumin and ground red pepper. Season to taste with salt and freshly ground black pepper. Simmer covered about 30 minutes. Taste to adjust seasonings.

4. Stir in the beans; add the corn if desired. Simmer uncovered about 10 minutes.

Terry's Brisket

Serves 6-8

TableTalk **featured Terry Hieken and her way of making this juicy brisket at a Hanukkah cooking class at the Missouri Botanical Garden.**

1 (4-5 pound) flat-cut brisket, frozen
1 tablespoon garlic powder, divided
1 tablespoon paprika, divided
Kosher salt and freshly ground pepper to taste
12 ounces frozen chopped onions or 1 pound fresh onions, • peeled and chopped
12 ounces beer

1. Preheat the oven to 425 degrees. Rinse the frozen brisket with cold water and pat it dry with paper towels. Place in a shallow pan, fat side up, and season well with half the garlic powder, paprika, salt and pepper.

2. Roast uncovered for 30 minutes. Turn, season the other side with remaining spices and roast another 30 minutes.

3. Turn the brisket fat side up, spread the onions in bottom of the pan, scraping up browned bits, pour on the beer and cover the pan closely with heavy-duty foil. Reduce the oven temperature to 350 degrees and cook another 2 to 3 hours until the meat is fork tender. After 2 hours, check every half hour to see if it needs more liquid. Warm water will do.

4. When fork tender, lift the meat out of the pan, wrap it in the foil and set aside or refrigerate if not serving immediately. Refrigerate the pan juices separately.

5. When the brisket is just cool enough to handle, cut off excess fat and slice the brisket across the grain. (Oven-hot or cold brisket is more difficult to slice.) Lift the fat off the pan juices. Place the brisket slices in a baking dish, spoon on some pan juices, cover with foil and reheat in a 300 degree oven about 30 minutes. Heat the remaining pan juices and serve on the side. Or serve the meat cold with horseradish.

Note:
Brisket can be sliced and frozen. Keep slices in their "order." Freeze pan juices separately.

• Do not use super sweet onions because they tend to caramelize too readily and burn.

Life in Vienna

When Helene and Sig Halpern talked about Vienna before World War II, they evoked a life bound by tradition and convention. Families lived in large apartment buildings, young couples dating met in front of the opera house and social life revolved around the coffee house.

Apartments were in four buildings surrounding a courtyard. Facing the street were the largest apartments. Those on the side were smaller and those in the rear, facing only the courtyard, were the smallest.

"But all the children in the building went to the same grade school, became friends and did homework together," Helene Halpern said. "You learned to be sensitive to other people's circumstances."

When couples were dating, the young man did not pick up his date at her apartment. They met in front of the opera or a museum, and not until an engagement was in the offing did a young woman introduce her fellow to her family.

"You met her parents and you were gone," Sig said.

The Viennese day began at seven or seven thirty with croissants and cocoa or coffee. Shortly after the first breakfast, the Viennese housewife went to the markets, taking her maid with her, if she had one. They went to the green grocer for produce, to the dairy store, the bakery, the butcher, the fishmonger and last to the delicatessen for out-of-season delicacies.

"Then they went home and cooked for three hours," Sig said.

At ten in the morning, it was time for second breakfast. Working people stopped for coffee and cake and school children ate the snack they had brought from home.

"We took sandwiches with us to school," Helene said. "Sometimes cheese, eggs, turnovers, or pâté. Sig said if they were really lucky, they got liver on bread.

At one in the afternoon, the entire family gathered at home for a feast of appetizers, soup, meat, vegetables, potatoes and dessert. Businesses and schools closed to make time for this ritual.

Around two or three in the afternoon, after a nap, fathers returned to work and children returned to school. But at four, there was another round of coffee and cake when businessmen met their friends at a coffee house.

"The meals at ten and four were to keep you from dying of hunger," Sig said. Helene said it was more of a social thing.

Offices closed at six and everyone went home for a light supper. Later in the evening, they returned to the coffee houses where adults met friends for cards or talk, and students met other students to study.

The summer Helene was fifteen, her mother sent her to Mrs. Schwartz's Finishing School where, with other young women, she learned to plan meals, shop for the ingredients, cook, set the table and arrange dinner parties.

"I learned a lot from Mrs. Schwartz," Helene said. "I was too young to go. Usually it was for eighteen year-olds. But I have so enjoyed cooking ever since, and I still use her cookbook."

Sig said he considered Helene's cooking American with Viennese flavors. "Her Hungarian Goulash is as American as beef stew," he said, "but the ingredients make it Viennese."

Helene's Hungarian Goulash

Serves 4-6

Helene Halpern's Goulash is a wonderful make-ahead dish that reheats nicely. In fact, it's best made the day ahead.

3 pounds stew beef, either chuck or shoulder, cut into 1½-inch cubes (Do not use round. It makes lean but flavorless stew.)
½ cup flour or more if needed
4 tablespoons vegetable oil, divided
Kosher salt and freshly ground pepper to taste
4 large onions, about 1½ pounds, peeled and finely chopped
2 garlic cloves, peeled and minced
1 tablespoon tomato paste
3 tablespoons sweet Hungarian paprika or ordinary paprika
½ cup water
1 cup canned sauerkraut
1 tablespoon caraway seeds
1 (12-ounce) package of broad noodles
1 teaspoon extra virgin olive oil

1. Preheat the oven to 325 degrees. Heat half the oil in a heavy ovenproof pan.

2. Put the flour in plastic bag and shake few pieces of meat at a time, shaking off excess flour. Brown the meat a few pieces at a time because meat will not brown in a crowded pan.

3. Remove the browned meat to a platter and season it to taste with salt and pepper. Continue browning the remaining meat.

4. Add the remaining oil to the pan. Stir in the onions and sauté them over moderate heat until translucent, about 5 minutes.

5. Stir in the garlic, tomato paste, paprika and water. Return the meat to the pan along with any juices. Cover and bake until the meat is fork tender, about 2 to 3 hours. Check every half hour. If the goulash appears dry, add a little warm water.

6. When the goulash is tender, cover the meat and refrigerate it. Refrigerate the gravy separately. Wash and dry the pan.

7. 45 minutes before serving, remove the fat from gravy. Return the gravy to the pan; stir in the sauerkraut and caraway seeds. Return the meat to pan. Simmer partly covered for 30 minutes.

8. While the goulash is cooking, boil the noodles. Drain and toss them with the olive oil to keep them from sticking. Serve the goulash over noodles.

Beef Stew

Serves 4-6

Don't let making stew scare you. Stew is the ultimate comfort food for the cook because almost all of it can be prepared in advance.

I prepare the meat portion of the stew a day or two before serving and then reheat it with freshly cooked vegetables. You can double the meat to prepare for two meals, starting with fresh vegetables for the second round.

The Meat
2 tablespoons vegetable oil
3 pounds stew beef, either chuck or shoulder, cut into 1½-inch cubes (If there is a bone, good. It adds depth and flavor to the stew. Do not use round. It makes lean but flavorless stew.)
¼ cup flour
Kosher salt and freshly ground pepper to taste
2 tablespoons extra virgin olive oil
2 large onions, sliced
1 tablespoon minced garlic
3 cups chicken, beef, or vegetable broth, water, wine or a combination
1 bay leaf
½ teaspoon thyme
1 medium tomato
1 tablespoon tomato paste
2 garlic cloves peeled but left whole

The Vegetables—Select any or all
4 large carrots, peeled, halved lengthwise and cut into chunks
2 large turnips, peeled and quartered
1 tablespoon extra virgin olive oil
6 small potatoes
Kosher salt and freshly ground pepper to taste
1 (10-ounce) package frozen peas
½ cup minced fresh parsley

The Meat

1. Preheat the oven to 325 degrees. Add the vegetable oil to a heavy ovenproof pan with a lid. Turn the heat to medium-high.

2. Put the flour in a plastic bag and shake a few pieces of the meat at a time, shaking off excess flour. Add the meat chunks to the pan a few at a time, turning them to brown on all sides. When all the meat is brown, remove it with a slotted spoon. If you have a beef bone, brown it, too. Salt and pepper the meat and set it aside.

3. Add the olive oil to the pan. Turn the heat to medium and sauté the onions until they soften, about 8 minutes. Add the garlic and sauté 2 minutes more.

4. Stir in the broth, bay leaf, thyme, tomato, tomato paste, garlic cloves and the meat and bones. Cover the pan and bring it to a simmer on top of the stove.

5. Put the pan in the oven and bake covered about 2½ hours, until the meat is fork tender. If the stew seems dry, add a little warm water. If the stew looks pale, remove the lid for 20-30 minutes while it is still in the oven.

6. Taste and adjust the seasoning. Remove the meat with a slotted spoon; wrap it well and refrigerate it.

7. Strain the gravy through a colander into a bowl, pressing out the juices from the vegetables. Discard these vegetables. Refrigerate the gravy; cover it when cool. When cold, lift off the fat and discard it.

The Vegetables

1. Put the carrots and turnips in a heavy pan. Add the oil, cover the pan and cook on medium heat until the vegetables are fork tender. Watch them so they do not burn.

2. Boil the potatoes, peeled or not. When tender, add them to the pot with the carrots and turnips. Season everything to taste with salt and pepper.

3. When ready to serve the stew, heat up the meat, the gravy and vegetables together. Add the peas and cook for 2 minutes. Taste to adjust seasoning and serve, garnished with parsley.

Beef Tenderloin

Serves 6-8

Beef tenderloin remains the king of meats. And it's easy to do for a crowd.

½ cup extra virgin olive oil
¼ cup minced fresh parsley
1 teaspoon fresh thyme sprigs or ½ teaspoon dried thyme
1 bay leaf
2 garlic cloves, lightly smashed
Kosher salt and freshly ground pepper to taste
1 (3-pound) beef tenderloin

1. Combine the oil, parsley, thyme, bay leaf, garlic, salt and pepper in a strong zip lock bag. Add the meat, zip the bag and refrigerate it for several hours.

2. Remove the meat from the refrigerator 1 hour before cooking, pat it dry with paper towels and put it in a shallow pan. Discard the marinade.

3. Place the oven rack about 4-5 inches from the broiler coils or flame. Preheat the oven to 450 degrees.

4. Roast the meat for 20 minutes. Change the heat source to broil, which will enhance its color. For very rare meat, remove after 5 minutes. Broil no more than 10 minutes. The meat thermometer will read about 125 degrees for medium rare.

5. Let the meat rest 5 minutes before slicing and serving with Tomato Chutney or horseradish.

Glazed Corned Beef

Serves 6

Glazed Corned Beef is good with hot mustard on rye bread or with eggs for breakfast.

1 (2½-3 pound) corned beef, preferably the flat cut
2 bay leaves
½ teaspoon mustard seeds
12 black peppercorns
½ cup mustard, any kind
¾ cup brown sugar
1-2 tablespoons water

1. Put the corned beef in a deep pot and add water to cover. Add the spice packet that comes with the corned beef, or add the bay leaves, mustard seeds and peppercorns. Bring to a boil, cover and simmer until fork tender, about 2-3 hours. When tender, place it on a cutting board.

2. As soon as it is cool enough to handle, slice it across the grain in thin or thick, slices, as you prefer. Reshape the slices of meat to look like the whole corned beef and wrap it tightly in foil. Refrigerate it until shortly before serving. Or freeze it, defrost it and continue with the recipe.

3. Preheat the oven to 350 degrees. Spread the mustard over the corned beef. Sprinkle with the brown sugar. Moisten the sugar with water as needed. Bake uncovered for 20 minutes or until the meat is hot and glazed.

Roast Rack of Lamb

Serves 4

For seventeen years, Billy and I have hosted cast parties for Opera Theatre of St. Louis, serving rack of lamb as the main dish. We cut the racks into 2-rib portions to be picked up and eaten without knives. We also offer pasta and salad, so that there is plenty for vegetarian opera singers.

2 racks of lamb
2 tablespoons extra virgin olive oil
1 teaspoon Kosher salt
¼ teaspoon freshly ground pepper
¼ cup minced fresh parsley leaves
1 teaspoon minced fresh garlic
1 teaspoon minced fresh rosemary leaves or ½ teaspoon dried
2 teaspoons Dijon mustard

1. The day before serving, remove excess fat from the racks, score the remaining fat with shallow cuts in a diamond pattern. Cut halfway down the bones between the chops.

2. Combine the remaining ingredients in a plastic bag. Add the racks to the bag, making sure the sauce covers them. Zip it closed and refrigerate until 1 hour before preparing.

3. Preheat the oven to 500 degrees.

4. Put the racks in the pan fat side up and roast about 20 minutes for medium-rare, 125 degrees on a meat thermometer.

5. Let the meat rest 5 minutes before carving. Serve with mint jelly or Tomato Chutney.

Mark Bittman Has Chutzpah·

Mark Bittman, author of *The Minimalist*, a weekly feature of the *New York Times* food page, had just published his tenth cookbook, *The Best Recipes in the World* (Broadway Books, 2005). The title reflects the chutzpah of one of his earlier books, *How to Cook Everything (Macmillan, 1998)*. With that kind of assuredness, the recipes have got to be good, and indeed they are.

Bittman was in St.Louis promoting the new book when the St. Louis Culinary Society nabbed him for a reception, and Billy and I nabbed the reception. Bittman is a beloved name in our kitchen, and we were happy to host him and the SLCS.

Bittman was born in 1950 (he looks younger) and grew up in New York "where there was always good food somewhere." He said his mother cooked simple meals in definite rotation…on Tuesday, it's…..and the whole family always sat down together for dinner.

He began his newspaper career writing free-lance food articles, some of which appeared in the *New York Times*. In 1997, he launched *The Minimalist* for the *Times*.

Bittman is funny and clever in the feature part of his columns, but his recipes make him invaluable. He has the ability to transform traditional recipes that are often complicated, making them clear and appealing.

• *Chutzpah* is Yiddish for *audacity* or *nerve*

Osso Buco

Adapted from *How to Cook Everything* by Mark Bittman (Macmillan, 1998)

Serves 4

Traditionally, Osso Buco is served with *Risotto Milanese*, but I prefer it with canned and drained Great Northern or cannellini beans.

4 large veal shanks, 8-12 ounces each
Flour for dredging
4 tablespoons extra virgin olive oil, divided
Kosher salt and freshly ground black pepper to taste
1 tablespoon minced garlic
3 anchovy fillets, minced
1 cup chopped onion
1 celery rib, chopped
2 medium carrots, peeled and chopped
1-2 sprigs fresh thyme or ½ teaspoon dried
¾ cup dry white wine
2 cups peeled, cored and chopped fresh or drained canned tomatoes
½ cup chicken, beef, vegetable broth or water

1. Preheat the oven to 350 degrees. Have ready a large ovenproof casserole with a lid that can hold all the shanks in one layer.

2. Wipe the shanks with a damp towel, pat them dry and dredge them in flour.

3. When the casserole is hot, add half the oil. When the oil is hot, shake off any excess flour on the shanks and add them to the casserole. Brown them well on all sides. Salt and pepper them to taste. Remove them to a plate.

4. Wipe out the casserole with paper towels. Turn the heat to medium and add the remaining oil. A minute later, add the garlic and anchovies. Cook and stir until the anchovies break up. Add the vegetables and thyme. Cook, stirring occasionally, until soft, about 10 minutes. Season the vegetables with salt and pepper.

5. Add the wine, turn the heat up a bit and let it bubble away for 1 minute.

6. Add the chopped tomatoes and cook until the mixture becomes saucy.

7. Nestle shanks among the vegetables and pour on the broth. Cover and bake for 1½-2 hours, turning the meat three or four times, until it is tender and almost falling off bones.

8. Refrigerate the meat and gravy separately. When cold, remove the fat and press the gravy through a strainer.

9. To serve, reheat the osso buco in the gravy. Serve it in large shallow soup bowls with small spoons or cocktail forks to extract the marrow. Add crusty bread to sop • up the sauce.

• The word "sop" comes from the French *soupe*, which originally referred to a piece of bread, boiled in porridge. Later, "sop" came to mean the piece of bread used to take up extra liquid.

Vegetables

Black Circle Series, detail
Waterless Lithography. 10" x 10".

Hotdog!

Marcella and Victor Hazan, celebrities by any standards, prefer being treated like ordinary people. (Marcella says people are afraid to invite them to dinner.) We go to their home for dinner. They come to ours. And they are in no way formidable guests. Victor helps Billy select the wine and makes the coffee in the Napoletana, the Italian coffee pot. And Marcella answers cooking questions.

But when it comes to the food, they comment only on what they like. If it is something not quite right, there is silence, and that's a comment, too.

Having them to dinner is a challenge we enjoy. They are charming guests and there is always good talk at the table. So as soon as we learned they loved kosher hotdogs and had not been able to find them in Sarasota, we invited them to share the hotdogs we had brought down to Florida from a deli in St.Louis—the kind in a long string made the old fashioned way.

Since they were our only guests, Marcella joined me in the kitchen, where things were not going well. I had slit the hot dogs before broiling them because they were so thick. But after only a few minutes, they turned black and curled up so much they would not fit on the buns. "Next time, slash them a few times so they will lie flat," Marcella said. And the buns! I had put them under the broiler to toast and forgot them until black smoke poured from the oven. I wanted to throw them out, but "No," said Marcella. "We'll scrape off the burn."

So we sat down to dinner with good red wine Victor suggested, (Marcella drinks only bourbon), with blackened hot dogs on blackened buns. The rest of the dinner was slaw, browned new potatoes and apple crisp. Victor said he liked the slaw because it had the right balance of sugar and vinegar. Marcella said nothing. Nor did they say a word about the rest of the dinner. There was that silence!

Marcella called the next day to thank us for the hotdog dinner. "I'll never forget them," she said. I asked her what Italian dish she would serve with hotdogs. She suggested Smothered Cabbage, Venetian Style.

Try it with your next hot dogs. Be sure to slash them first, and don't burn the buns.

Smothered Cabbage Venetian Style

Adapted from *Essentials of Classic Italian Cooking* by Marcella Hazan (Alfred A. Knopf, 1997)

Serves 6

2 pounds green, red or Savoy cabbage
½ cup chopped onion
½ cup extra virgin olive oil
1 tablespoon chopped garlic
Kosher salt and freshly ground black pepper to taste
1 tablespoon red wine vinegar

1. Shred the cabbage. A food processor works well. Set aside.

2. Put the onion and oil in a deep sauté pan and sauté the onion on medium heat until it becomes golden.

3. Add the garlic and sauté it for 2 minutes until it becomes a pale gold, and then add the cabbage. Stir and turn it for several minutes until it wilts.

4. Stir in the salt, pepper and the vinegar. Cover the pan and turn the heat down to low. Cook about 1½ hours or until the cabbage is very tender, stirring every so often. If the cabbage seems dry, add 2 tablespoons water as needed.

5. When done, taste and correct for salt and pepper. Allow it to settle a few minutes off the heat before serving.

Roasted Asparagus

Serves 4-6

Roasted Asparagus, good with chicken, fish, meat or a salad, can be served hot or at room temperature.

2 pounds medium asparagus, washed, rough ends snapped off, stalks trimmed
   and peeled if desired
¼ cup extra virgin olive oil
1 teaspoon kosher salt
¼ teaspoon freshly ground black pepper

1. Preheat the oven to 450 degrees. Put the asparagus in a roasting pan with oil, salt and pepper. Shake the pan to coat them evenly with the oil and seasonings.

2. Roast until the asparagus are softened but retain some crunch, 10-12 minutes.

Quick Pickled Beets

Adapted from *How to Cook Everything* by Mark Bittman (Macmillan, 1998)

Serves 4-6

This is the recipe for beet lovers. It's good with meats or chicken.

2 pounds beets
2 cups white vinegar
1 cup sugar
2 tablespoons kosher salt
1 teaspoon allspice berries
¼ teaspoon cloves
½ cinnamon stick, optional
1 medium onion, peeled and sliced

1. Preheat the oven to 400 degrees. Remove all but 1 inch of beet greens. Scrub and dry the beets and wrap them individually in foil. Place them in a pan and bake 1 hour or until a sharp knife easily pierces the beets right through the foil. Set them aside and refrigerate until ready to prepare pickled beets. The foil-wrapped beets can be refrigerated for several days.

2. The peels of cooked beets slip off easily. Peel them and slice them ⅛-¼-inch thick.

3. Bring the vinegar, sugar, salt and spices to a boil. Add the beets and onions and cook about 1 minute. Cool, refrigerate and eat within 2 weeks.

Butternut Squash with Red Bell Pepper

Serves 6-8

This vegetarian casserole has an appealing combination of flavors, and it's easy to prepare, once you have peeled the squash.

3½ pounds butternut squash
1 large red bell pepper, seeded and diced into 1-inch pieces
3 tablespoons extra virgin olive oil
2 large garlic cloves, minced
3 tablespoons minced fresh parsley
1½ teaspoons minced fresh rosemary or ½ teaspoon dried
1 teaspoon kosher salt or more to taste and freshly ground pepper to taste
½ cup freshly grated Parmesan cheese

1. Preheat the oven to 400 degrees.

2. Peel the squash by cutting it into halves and then into fourths, discarding the seeds. Use a vegetable peeler to peel each section down to the orange flesh. Slice into 1-inch cubes.

3. Combine the squash with everything but the Parmesan cheese in a 9x13-inch baking pan.

4. At this point, the casserole can be refrigerated to bake later. Bring it to room temperature one hour before baking.

5. Sprinkle with the Parmesan cheese. Bake in the middle shelf of the oven until the vegetables are tender and the top is golden, about 1 hour. Serve at once.

Corn on the Cob

Years ago, corn had to be cooked and eaten the moment it was picked. If you waited too long, the corn's sugar turned to starch and the flavor was gone. Today, scientists have developed corn that maintains its sugar for several days, thus giving it a longer shelf life.

Taking Care Of Corn

Don't shuck the corn until you are ready to cook it. Keep the ears refrigerated in a plastic bag, and tuck in some wet paper towels to keep them from drying. Use the corn within 1-2 days.

Boiling

This method is good if you have lots of corn to cook. Shuck it right before cooking.

1. Fill a large pot (or pots) with 4-6 quarts of water.

2. Bring the water to a boil. Drop in the corn.

3. When the water returns to a boil, take the pot off the heat and let the corn remain in the water for 5 minutes. It's ready. It can stay in the water an extra 5-10 minutes if you aren't ready.

Steaming

This method is good if you have 8 ears or less to prepare. I think steaming enhances the flavor of the corn. Shuck it right before cooking.

1. Put an inch of water in the bottom of a large pot. Bring it to a boil.

2. Place the corn in 1 layer if possible in a steamer basket or metal colander or a rack, whatever will keep the corn out of the water and allow you to close the lid.

3. Steam the corn for 10 minutes. Take the pot off the heat. The corn can wait for you for 5-10 minutes.

4. While the corn is steaming, make sure the water does not boil out of the pot.

Roasted Corn with Red Peppers and Scallions

Serves 4

This is a superb side dish, especially if you have excellent corn.

4 ears of corn, shucked
2 tablespoons extra virgin olive oil
1 garlic clove, minced
1 large red bell pepper, finely diced
6 scallions, diced
1 teaspoon ground cumin
Kosher salt and freshly ground black pepper to taste
¼ cup fresh minced parsley

1. Hold a cob on end over a clean towel. To keep the kernels from scattering, strip the kernels from the middle of the cob down. Reverse the cob and strip off the rest of the kernels.

2. Put the oil in large skillet that can take high heat, like cast iron. Turn the heat to high. Add the corn and cook, shaking the pan or stirring occasionally, until the corn is lightly charred, about 5-7 minutes. Add the garlic, red peppers and scallions; cook and stir for 2 minutes more.

3. Take the pan off the heat. Season to taste with cumin, salt and pepper. Toss with parsley and serve.

Green Beans Hot or Cold

Serves 4

Taste a raw bean in the market. If it has no flavor, use broccoli. There are two recipes here—one for hot beans with butter and one for room temperature beans with olive oil.

1½ pounds good tasting green beans
6 quarts water
1½ tablespoons kosher salt plus more for seasoning cooked beans
2 tablespoons melted butter or 2 tablespoons extra virgin olive oil
Freshly ground pepper
3 tablespoons white sesame seeds, optional

1. Trim the stem ends of the beans. Rinse. Bring the water to a boil. Add the salt. Add the beans.

2. When the water returns to boil, time the beans. About 5 minutes should be enough. Taste one to see if it is done the way you like it. Drain them and serve them at once with melted butter and salt and pepper to taste.

3. To serve at room temperature, have a bowl of ice water ready. Put the cooked beans into the cold water to stop the cooking and maintain their bright color. Drain them and dry them on terrycloth towels.

4. Put the beans in large bowl. Toss with salt and pepper to taste and the olive oil. Toss with sesame seeds.

Notes:

1. Cauliflower, sugar snaps and snow peas can be prepared and served the same way. The timing on each vegetable will be slightly different. The cauliflower will take about 8 minutes, the snaps and peas, maybe 3. Taste to see if they are done the way you wish them.

2. Vegetables seasoned with olive oil taste good the next day. Just add a little more seasoning, a few drops of good wine vinegar and you have a salad.

Culinary Travelers

We had planned our trip to Italy in October around a special session on the foods of Venice with Marcella Hazan. But before Venice, our own culinary tour took us to Milan where we first tasted fresh wild porcini mushrooms. Highly prized by Italians who prefer them to cultivated white mushrooms, boletus edulis grow in forests in late spring and again in September and October, when they are served in restaurants and sold at roadside stands near where they are gathered.

We ate them whenever they were on the menu. In Milan, they were sautéed in butter and floated in rich chicken broth. In Stresa, on the western bank of Lake Maggiore, they were grilled with olive oil and garlic and served over shredded arugula. In Asolo, a small hill town northwest of Venice, they were sautéed in butter and added to risotto.

After Asolo, we joined Marcella Hazan and her husband, Victor, an Italian wine expert, and fifteen others like ourselves in Venice where Marcella took us behind the scenes of Venetian cooking as the program had promised.

Early one morning, we toured the markets on the far side of the Rialto Bridge where fish must still be moving for Venetians to consider them fresh enough to purchase. Near the fish were the vegetable stalls where produce is fresh as the fish and displayed in a blaze of color. Marcella said that Venetians never plan the day's meals before they see what the market offers.

Victor suggested a shop near the Rialto Bridge that sold high quality dried porcini mushrooms. Dried porcini are in no way a second-best substitute for fresh. What is lost in moistness and texture is more than compensated for in a musky, earthy flavor, reminiscent of the forest they came from. And while they are relatively expensive, a small amount combined with white cultivated mushrooms floods them with their flavor. Furthermore, dried porcini can be in season every month of the year because they keep indefinitely in a well-sealed bag in the refrigerator.

The Hazans took us by launch to a restaurant on Torcello, one of the islands in the Venetian lagoon about one hour from St. Mark's Square, where we ate fifteen different kinds of fish from the Adriatic. Another day, we drank wines in a vineyard in Friuli, a wine section of Italy north of Venice. We had lunch in an old inn where one of the seven courses was puréed bean soup thick with barley. That night, we skipped dinner.

For thirteen days, we dined superbly. Even the food on the returning air trip was excellent, because it had been prepared in Italy. And though we ate heartily at every meal, except for the supper we skipped, we did not return pounds heavier. The cuisine is based mainly on lean grains and vegetables instead of meats, and while there are many courses, portions are small. There is no butter on the table to accompany that wonderfully dense bread, and oils and butters never dominate the dishes and mask the flavors of the fresh seasonal foods so dear to Italians.

Three Mushroom Ragout

Serves 4

The Ragout, dominated by the woodsy flavor of dried porcini, is a good side dish with chicken or meats.

1 ounce dried porcini mushrooms
1½ cups warm water
1 pound fresh shitake mushrooms
1 pound fresh white mushrooms
2 tablespoons extra virgin olive oil
2 tablespoons minced shallots
1 cup dry white wine
½ cup cream
Kosher salt and freshly ground pepper to taste
3 tablespoons minced fresh parsley

1. Soak the porcini in warm tap water at least 30 minutes. Set a strainer lined with a coffee filter over a bowl. Lift the porcini out of the water. Pour the soaking liquid through the filter and reserve it. Wash the porcini thoroughly under cold running water to get rid of any sand or grit. Chop them coarsely and set aside.

2. Rinse the shitake mushroom quickly under cold running water. Dry them on terrycloth towels. Remove and discard the stems. Set them aside.

3. Rinse the white mushrooms quickly under cold running water. Dry them on terrycloth towels. Cut them in half or quarter them if large. Set them aside.

4. Put the oil and shallots into a heavy sauté pan. Sauté the shallots until they are yellow and faintly transparent. Add the wine. Raise the heat and cook until almost all the wine has evaporated.

5. Add the reconstituted mushrooms and their soaking liquid. Raise the heat and cook uncovered until almost all the liquid has evaporated.

6. Add the fresh mushrooms. Cover and cook slowly until the mushrooms have released their liquid. Then raise the heat and cook uncovered until almost all this liquid has evaporated.

7. Stir in the cream and cook until the mixture has thickened a little. Season to taste with salt and pepper. Sprinkle with parsley and serve.

Poverty Fries

Serves 4

This recipe appeared in an article I wrote for the *Post-Dispatch* on living on food stamps. Jim Firestone thought the name fit both the potatoes and the story.

4 large unpeeled baking potatoes or peeled sweet potatoes
1 tablespoon extra virgin olive oil
1 tablespoon water
Kosher salt to taste

1. Preheat the oven to 400 degrees. Scrub the potatoes and cut as for French fries.

2. Toss them with oil and water. Put them in a baking pan with sides. Bake, turning potatoes after 20 minutes. Continue baking about 20 minutes more or until the potatoes are brown and crisp. Salt and serve at once.

Potato Pancakes

Serves 4

Inspired by Sharon Baizer Winstein, these latkes are the favorites at our Hanukkah dinners.

1¼ pounds baking potatoes, peeled and shredded or 2 ½ cups purchased
   shredded potatoes
1 medium onion, shredded
2 tablespoons flour
2 eggs
¾ teaspoon kosher salt
⅛ teaspoon freshly ground pepper
½ cup canola or extra virgin olive oil plus more as needed

1. Toss the potatoes and onions with the flour. Stir in the eggs, salt and pepper.

2. Heat the oil in a skillet on medium high heat.

3. Stir the batter before forming each pancake. Drop about 2 tablespoons of batter for each pancake into the skillet, allowing space between the pancakes. With the back of a spoon, shape them into 3-inch rounds.

4. Sauté the pancakes about 4-5 minutes on the first side, until the edges are brown. Turn them and cook about 4 minutes more, regulating the heat so they cook through but do not burn.

5. Drain them on paper towels. Serve immediately. To serve later, reheat them in a 350 degree oven for 10 minutes.

Creamed Spinach

Serves 4-6

Inspired by Julia Child, this wonderful spinach is also good and slightly leaner using evaporated milk instead of cream and without the final butter.

2 (10-ounce) boxes frozen chopped spinach
3 tablespoons butter
½ teaspoon kosher salt
Pinch of freshly ground pepper
Pinch of nutmeg
1½ tablespoons flour
1 cup whipping cream or 1 cup evaporated milk, divided (You may not need all of it.)
Powdered sugar, optional
1-2 tablespoons softened butter, optional

1. Place the unwrapped frozen spinach on a large cutting board. When it is partially defrosted, slice it into chunks.

2. Melt the butter in a heavy saucepan. Stir in the spinach, salt, pepper and nutmeg. Cover and cook very slowly until the spinach has thawed and released its juices, about 5 minutes or so.

3. Uncover the pan, raise the heat and stir until all the moisture has evaporated, about 3-5 minutes.

4. Sift the flour onto the spinach. Turn the heat to medium and stir continuously for 2 minutes.

5. Remove the pan from the heat and stir in about two thirds of the cream spoonful by spoonful, stirring continuously. Bring it to simmer, cover, and cook very slowly about 5 minutes, stirring frequently. If the spinach seems dry, add more cream by spoonfuls. Taste to adjust the seasoning with salt, pepper, nutmeg or teaspoons of powdered sugar.

6. If not to be served immediately, set aside uncovered and film the top with a tablespoon of cream. To serve, stir in the softened butter and reheat.

Sweet Potatoes

Serves 6- 8

A friend brought these to one of our Thanksgiving celebrations, and we have made them standard fare.

2 pounds sweet potatoes, peeled and sliced ¼-inch thick, about 4 cups
2 pounds tart apples, peeled, cored and sliced ¼-inch thick, about 4 cups
1 cup sugar
1 cup cold water
2 tablespoons cornstarch
½ cup (1 stick) butter

1. Preheat the oven to 350 degrees. Layer the potatoes and apples in a 2-quart baking dish.

2. Combine the sugar, water, cornstarch and butter in a small saucepan. Stir and cook over medium heat until the sugar has dissolved and the butter has melted. Pour it over the potatoes and apples.

3. Bake uncovered about 1½ hours, until the potatoes and apples are tender and the casserole is starting to brown.

Roasted Vegetables

Serves 4

This recipe can be increased easily, though you may have to roast them in several batches. They are best prepared shortly before serving but can be done early, refrigerated and reheated in a microwave. Garnish pasta with leftover vegetables or make them into sandwiches.

2 pounds fresh vegetables such as zucchini, yellow squash, red, yellow and orange
    bell peppers, asparagus, scallions, small yellow onions and red onions
4 garlic cloves, peeled and minced
1 tablespoon fresh thyme or 1 teaspoon dried
¼ cup balsamic vinegar
3 tablespoons extra virgin olive oil
Kosher salt and freshly ground pepper to taste
3 tablespoons minced fresh parsley

1. Preheat the oven to 375 degrees. Scrub and halve the zucchini and yellow squash lengthwise. Clean and quarter the peppers. Trim the asparagus and scallions. Peel the onions and quarter them if large.

2. Combine the garlic, thyme, vinegar, oil, salt and pepper in a large bowl. Add the prepared vegetables and toss to coat them with the marinade.

3. Place the vegetables in a single layer in a baking pan. Bake them about 30 minutes or until they are soft. Toss with parsley and serve.

4. Or grill the vegetables about 5 minutes on each side. Toss with parsley and serve.

The Gifts of Summer

My father was not gracious about receiving gifts. He would reluctantly open a package bedecked with ribbons, glance at what it contained and set it aside with a small "thank you." Mother must have done something with those ties, sweaters and shirts because we never saw them again.

But come late July and early August, if we were to bring him a basket of tomatoes from a farmer's market, his face lit up with gratitude and anticipation.

He would bite into a tomato as though it were an apple, sprinkle on a little salt and enjoy what was for him the best of all possible gifts. And not only did he love summer tomatoes, he loved them pale red and cold from the refrigerator.

(I inherited his love of summer tomatoes. I love them cold from the refrigerator, despite what food experts say, though I do prefer them ripe red.)

While markets have gorgeous tomatoes all year, those beauties have been bred to withstand shipping and a long shelf life, and along the way, have lost that summer aroma and flavor that make a tomato a tomato.

But come July, August and September, even large chain markets feature home grown tomatoes from nearby farmers, and farmers' markets are stocked with tomatoes of every variety. Slice them with fresh basil and sweet onion rings or toss them with sour cream for Farmer's Chop Suey. Or make Crostini with Tomatoes and Basil, Tomato Soup or My Gazpacho. For a year-round treat, try Stewed Tomatoes or Tomato Chutney. Don't pass up the gifts of summer.

Stewed Tomatoes

Makes about 4 cups

In December, they remind us of August.

4 pounds ripe tomatoes
4 tablespoons butter
½ cup finely chopped onion, optional
Kosher salt and freshly ground pepper to taste
1 teaspoon sugar or to taste
2 tablespoons chopped fresh basil, optional
Crackers crumbled to thicken the tomatoes, optional

1. Drop the tomatoes into boiling water for 10-15 seconds. Remove with slotted spoon. Peel and core them at once or refrigerate them to peel and core later.

2. Chop the peeled and cored tomatoes into quarters. Put them in a heavy skillet with butter and optional onion. Cover and cook slowly until the tomatoes break down, about 10 minutes. Add salt, pepper and sugar. Cook uncovered on medium heat 10 minutes more. Stir in basil and crumbled crackers, if desired.

3. Serve immediately or freeze to use later as is or to add to soups, stews or chili.

Tomato Chutney

Makes 5-6 cups

Chef Bill Cardwell of Cardwell's at the Plaza gave me this recipe when I first interviewed him in 1989. It's a good relish with meats or chicken.

2 pounds tomatoes
2 large red onions, coarsely chopped
1 fresh jalapeño pepper with seeds, minced
1 tablespoon minced fresh garlic
1 tablespoon peeled and minced fresh ginger
1 cup red wine vinegar
1 cup firmly packed brown sugar
1 cup light corn syrup
1 (6-ounce) can tomato paste
2 teaspoons kosher salt
1 teaspoon white pepper
1 teaspoon cinnamon
¼ teaspoon ground cloves
½ teaspoon mace
2 tablespoons minced fresh cilantro
1 tablespoon minced fresh mint leaves

1. Peel the tomatoes by dropping them into boiling water for 10 seconds. Remove them with a slotted spoon and peel them immediately or refrigerate them to peel later. To seed and juice them, slice them in half crosswise and squeeze out the seeds and juice. Coarsely chop them.

2. Combine everything but the cilantro and mint in a deep microwave dish.

3. Microwave on high for about 50 minutes, stirring every 10 minutes, until the chutney is thick.

4. Stir in the cilantro and mint. Chill and freeze.

Sweets

Black Circle Series, *detail*
Waterless Lithography and Collage. 10" x 10".

Love Food

While no one has yet established scientifically that foods can inspire love and devotion, no one would disagree that good food gladdens the eye, the heart and the rest of the body. Food is not only the sustenance of life; it can also be its spice. And for many people, that spice is chocolate.

The Aztecs were the first to appreciate chocolate—they believed it was an aphrodisiac. Montezuma, the last Aztec emperor of Mexico, reportedly drank 50 cups of chocolate a day. In the French court, royalty offered chocolate to their ladies in hopes of gaining favors. Men send their sweethearts chocolates, and young girls bake brownies for their boy friends. It is probably the world's best-loved flavor, at least according to the movie, *Chocolat*.

The magical power of chocolate is the theme of *Chocolat,* starring Juliette Binoche as Vianne Rocher, a free-spirited young beautiful woman who opens a chocolate shop in a small French village sometime in the early 20th century. The camera focuses on melted chocolate swirling and glistening in the pan, chocolate creams and truffles rolled in cocoa. Miss Binoche even sports a chocolate-colored mole on the left side of her neck. Sales of chocolate in the lobby must have doubled when the movie was playing.

But the best chocolate in the movie is the pot of hot chocolate Mademoiselle Rocher offers everyone who passes by. One sip and they feel better. They smile; they glow and they want to know what's in it. Mademoiselle Rocher tells them it's only hot chocolate laced with a little hot pepper.

This French lady probably did not know why the hot pepper acted the way it did. It's only lately that scientists have made important discoveries about hot peppers. What makes them hot is capsaicin, and there is now some evidence that capsaicin in hot peppers, added to foods like soups and the movie's hot chocolate, may lessen colds, sinus infections and migraine headaches.

Therefore, to add spice to a relationship, and at the same time make your love feel better if he or she has upper respiratory problems, offer hot chocolate with pepper. It may or may not be an aphrodisiac, but no one will deny that it is a love potion.

Peppered Hot Chocolate

Serves 2

Inspired by the movie *Chocolat*, pepper enhances the flavor and warmth of hot chocolate.

2 cups milk (can be part cream)
4 ounces bittersweet chocolate, chopped
¾ teaspoon cinnamon
Pinch cayenne pepper or to taste

1. In a small saucepan, heat the milk to a bare simmer.

2. On low heat, whisk the chopped chocolate into the milk until the mixture is smooth. Remove from the heat.

3. Stir in the cinnamon and pepper to taste. Careful with cayenne pepper. It's hot.

Dream Cake

Serves 10

This cake is a special treat.

8 ounces semisweet chocolate
1 cup (2 sticks) butter
1 cup sugar
½ cup prepared coffee
4 eggs
Powdered sugar, ice cream or fresh raspberries to garnish

1. Preheat the oven to 350 degrees. Grease a 9-inch spring form pan. Line it with foil and set the pan aside.

2. In a double boiler or microwave, melt the chocolate with the butter and sugar.

3. When the mixture is cool, beat in the coffee. Beat in the eggs one at a time. Pour into the prepared pan.

4. Set the pan on top of a cookie sheet and bake 30 minutes or until a crust forms on top. A toothpick inserted in the cake will come out crumbly but not wet.

5. Cool the cake in the pan on a rack and when cool, refrigerate it. Keep the cake refrigerated in the pan and serve within 5 days or freeze it.

6. To serve, cut the cake into small slices. Dust with powdered sugar or add a scoop of ice cream on the side with a few fresh raspberries.

Chocolate Chewies

Makes about 2½ dozen cookies

I found this recipe in a magazine at the dentist's office. Later, I saw it in a cookbook. Maybe the cookbook author and I go to the same dentist.

3 cups powdered sugar •
½ cup unsweetened cocoa
2 tablespoons flour •
3 egg whites
2 cups coarsely chopped pecans ••

1. Preheat the oven to 350 degrees. Grease 2 cookie sheets or line them with parchment paper.

2. Slowly blend the sugar, cocoa and flour in an electric mixer.

3. Beat in the egg whites one at a time. Then beat at high speed for 1 minute. Stir in the pecans.

4. Use a rounded tablespoon of batter for each cookie, allowing 2 inches between cookies. Bake 15 minutes, switching the sheets on the shelves after 8 minutes. Cool the cookies on the baking sheet a few minutes and then transfer them to racks.

• For Passover, replace the powdered sugar with 1 cup granulated sugar. Replace the flour with the same amount of potato starch. The directions remain the same.

•• Taste the pecans. If lacking flavor, toast them in a 300 degree oven on a dry cookie sheet for 20 minutes. Chop when cool.

She Cooks for Comfort

Marion Burros, *New York Times* columnist and author of 13 cookbooks, was in St. Louis to talk about her latest book, *Cooking for Comfort* (Simon & Schuster, 2003), begun after September 11, 2001. She said comfort foods, though they may differ for everyone, remind each of us of simpler times when someone took care of us and kept us safe. "It's what we turn to in times of stress," she said. "Comfort foods are good for you physiologically and emotionally."

Burros and I met for breakfast in the dining room of the Ritz-Carlton Hotel, where she ordered what may be the newest comfort food—hot milk with tea. After some hesitation at the unusual order, the waitress brought her a pot of steaming milk and some Earl Grey tea bags that Burros dipped into the milk until it was a creamy tan. "I like milk in my tea, and this is what evolved," she said.

The milk and tea must have done the trick, because she appeared completely comfortable and relaxed, even though she had been flying around the country to promote her book. She was going to speak to The Women's Democratic Forum of Greater St. Louis at noon and then fly to the next city on her tour in late afternoon.

Burros said that more young people are cooking today. "This is the generation whose parents did not cook, but kids are cooking. It is a form of rebellion that they are cooking, looking at what they missed. Furthermore, women are attracted to men who cook. I have a friend whose son is a cook, and girls are flocking to him, much as if he were walking a dog."

Cooking and entertaining at home has become more popular since 9/11, she said. "In times of stress, people like to 'nest.' People in New York are carrying out food from expensive restaurants and entertaining at home. They are more comfortable at home, where they might cook one thing and buy the rest."

Soft Chocolate Chip Cookies

Adapted from *Cooking for Comfort* by Marion Burros (Simon & Schuster, 2003)

Makes 5-6 dozen

These are elegant chocolate chip cookies, especially when made with fine chocolate.

1 cup (2 sticks) butter, softened
¾ cup packed dark brown sugar
¾ cup sugar
2 eggs
1 teaspoon vanilla
2¼ cups flour
2 teaspoons powdered instant espresso coffee
1 teaspoon baking soda
½ teaspoon salt
12 ounces bittersweet chocolate, coarsely chopped, or 12 ounces chocolate
  chunks
1 cup chopped pecans, optional •

1. Place the racks near the middle of the oven. Preheat the oven to 375 degrees. Grease 2 baking sheets or line them with parchment paper.

2. Cream the butter with the sugars. Add the eggs, one at a time, beating well after each addition. Add vanilla and mix well.

3. Whisk the flour with the espresso, baking soda and salt. Slowly add it to the mixing bowl. Stir in the chocolate and optional pecans.

4. Drop the dough by heaping teaspoonfuls onto the baking sheets, allowing 2 inches between cookies. For flatter cookies, pat the dough with the back of a spoon before baking. Bake 8 to 10 minutes, reversing sheets on shelves after 5 minutes. Let the cookies cool a few minutes on the baking sheets and then transfer them to racks.

• Taste pecans. If lacking flavor, toast them in a 300 degree oven on a dry cookie sheet for 20 minutes. Chop when cool.

Double Chips

Makes about 5 dozen

My first *TableTalk* in 1995 featured Hortense Morgan and her Double Chips that she baked for charities. They are enormously popular.

1 cup (2 sticks) butter
¾ cup sugar
2 teaspoons vanilla
1¾ cups flour
1 cup semisweet chocolate chunks or chocolate chips
1 (4-ounce) bag potato chips, coarsely crushed in the bag
Powdered sugar to sift on finished cookies

1. Preheat the oven to 350 degrees.

2. Cream the butter with sugar and vanilla. Stir in the flour and chocolate chunks.

3. Lightly mix in crushed potato chips. (Some potato chips may stick out of the dough.)

4. Drop the dough by teaspoonful onto ungreased cookie sheets, allowing an inch between cookies. Bake 15 to 20 minutes, switching sheets on shelves after 8 minutes. Bake until cookies are just beginning to brown. Remove the cookies from the cookie sheets to a heavy towel.

5. While hot, sift powdered sugar over them. When cool, sift on additional powdered sugar. Store in tins or freeze.

Best Brownies

Makes 16 (2-inch) brownies

These are prize brownies.

½ cup (1 stick) butter
2 eggs
1¼ cups sugar
1 teaspoon vanilla
¾ cup flour
¼ cup unsweetened cocoa
Powdered sugar to garnish

1. Preheat the oven to 350 degrees. Grease and flour an 8x8-inch baking pan.

2. Melt the butter. Set it aside to cool.

3. Beat the eggs with the sugar.

4. Stir the cooled butter and vanilla into the eggs.

5. Combine the flour and cocoa and stir into the mixture. Do not over mix.

6. Spread in the prepared pan. Bake in the top half of the oven for about 20 minutes, until the center is firm to the touch.

7. When cool, cut into squares and sift powdered sugar on top.

Once a Foodie...

I don't know if there was such a word as "foodie" when I was a child, but if so, I would have qualified.

Long before I started playing in the kitchen, I was playing in the sandbox. Where my friends made castles, mountains and valleys, I made cakes, pies and cookies.

I read nursery rhymes in which good English children had bread and milk for supper, served by nanny in the nursery. How good it sounded. I begged Mother for bread and milk, even though we had no nanny and no nursery. She said I wouldn't like it, and indeed, she was right.

Reading Johanna Spyri's *Heidi* was both literary and culinary pleasure. Do you remember the fresh goat cheese that Grandfather melted onto dark bread for Heidi? And do you remember the goat's milk that made Heidi's friend Clara walk again?

And then there is Charles Dickens. Here was an author who knew the value of food. The turkey in *A Christmas Carol*, the largest one in the market, was the culmination of Scrooge's transformation and redemption.

But my favorite food story is by I. B. Singer. In his short story, *The Spinoza of Market Street*, old, toothless and scholarly Dr. Fischelson is slowly dying of poverty and ulcers when he meets Black Dobbe, a tall skinny old maid who cooks soup and kasha in milk for him. His health improves, they marry, the wedding guests eat cookies with their vodka, and, much to his surprise and joy, Dr. Fischelson consummates his marriage.

Movies are for foodies, too. My favorite is *Babette's Feast*, in which exquisite French food brings peace to disgruntled people. Another favorite is *Eat Drink Man Woman*. The Chinese food will send you to a Chinese restaurant before the credits run. *Tortilla Soup* is *Eat Drink Man Woman* moved to Mexico. It's not as good as its predecessor, but it's worth it for the shots of Mexican food and for Martin's Porcupines.

Martin's Porcupines

Inspired by *Tortilla Soup*

Makes about 2 dozen cookies

1 cup pecans
1 tablespoon unsalted butter, melted
2½ cups sweetened shredded coconut
½ cup chopped dried apricots
½ cup chopped semisweet chocolate or chocolate morsels
1 (14-ounce) can sweetened condensed milk

1. Preheat the oven to 325 degrees. Line a cookie sheet with parchment paper.

2. Toss the pecans in melted butter. Spread them in an ungreased pan and bake 10 to 15 minutes or until golden and aromatic. Let them cool and then chop them coarsely and combine them with the remaining ingredients.

3. Spoon about 2 tablespoons of batter for each cookie onto the cookie sheet and flatten to 2¼ inches in diameter. Allow 2 inches between cookies.

4. Bake about 10 minutes or until the coconut turns pale gold. Don't let the cookies brown. Transfer them to racks to cool.

Sandwich Cookies

Makes about 4 dozen 2-inch cookies

Aunt Hilda taught Mother and Mother taught me to make these unusual cookies. The dough is one of the easiest to roll.

4 eggs
3 cups flour
1 cup sugar
1 cup (2 sticks) butter, cold
3 eggs
1 egg white, slightly beaten
1 12-ounce jar raspberry preserves

1. Preheat the oven to 350 degrees. Separate 4 of the eggs, reserving whites for another use. Drop the 4 yolks into boiling water. Cook until firm, about 6 minutes. Drain on paper towels.

2. Pulverize the cooked yolks with flour in a food processor. Add the sugar. Cut the butter into small pieces; add to the flour mixture and process until small crumbs form.

3. Separate the 3 eggs. Reserve the whites for glazing the cookie tops. Add the 3 raw yolks to the processor and mix until blended.

4. Roll the dough about ⅛-inch thick. Cut out circles or hearts. In half of them, which will be tops of the sandwiches, cut holes in the centers with a thimble.

5. Brush the tops with egg white. Bake 6-8 minutes until the cookies start to brown.

6. Remove them from the cookie sheets to racks. When cool, spread the bottoms with about 1 teaspoon raspberry preserves. Press on the tops with a light twisting motion.

Poppy Seed Cookies

Makes 7-9 dozen cookies

These were a Grandma Peskind specialty. They are perfect with a cup of hot tea.

3 eggs
1 cup plus 3 tablespoons sugar for tops
½ cup extra virgin olive or vegetable oil plus 2 tablespoons to brush cookie tops
½ teaspoon salt
4 cups flour
3 tablespoons poppy seeds
1 teaspoon cinnamon

1. Preheat the oven to 350 degrees. Grease the cookie sheets.

2. Beat the eggs. Gradually, mix in 1 cup sugar. Add ½ cup oil, salt, flour and poppy seeds. Mix thoroughly.

3. Combine the remaining sugar with cinnamon. Set aside.

4. Divide the dough into small portions. Roll out one portion at a time on well-floured waxed paper until the dough is as thin as possible. Invert the waxed paper with the dough onto a prepared cookie sheet. Carefully, peel off the waxed paper and discard.

5. Brush the dough with oil and sprinkle it with the sugar-cinnamon mixture. With a knife, mark the dough with shallow vertical cuts in 2-inch columns. Then make shallow cuts on the diagonal, creating diamond-shaped cookies. There will always be a few oddly shaped cookies.

6. Repeat with the remaining dough, using fresh waxed paper each time.

7. Bake 10 to 12 minutes or until the cookies are light brown. Separate cookies where cut and immediately cool them on racks. They will crisp as they cool.

Oatmeal Lace Cookies

Makes 2-3 dozen

These are for crisp oatmeal cookies lovers.

½ cup (1 stick) butter, melted and cooled
1½ cups quick or old-fashioned oats (not instant)
1 egg, beaten
½ cup sugar
¼ cup firmly packed brown sugar
1 tablespoon flour
1 teaspoon baking powder
⅛ teaspoon salt
1 cup chopped pecans •
1 teaspoon vanilla

1. Combine the cooled butter with the oatmeal. Stir in the egg, sugars, flour, baking powder and salt.

2. Stir in the chopped pecans and vanilla. Refrigerate the dough overnight or until it is firm enough to roll into balls.

3. Preheat the oven to 350 degrees. Line cookie sheets with foil. Place walnut-sized balls of dough on the foil with at least 3 inches between them. Press each cookie down with a fork.

4. Bake 10-12 minutes. Let them stay on the foil for 4 minutes. Then remove them from the foil to cool on racks.

• Taste the pecans. If lacking flavor, toast them in a 300-degree oven on a dry cookie sheet for 20 minutes. Chop when cool.

Oatmeal Cookies

Makes about 5-6 dozen small cookies

Old-fashioned and good, they are Billy's favorites.

1 cup raisins
1 cup (2 sticks) butter
1 cup sugar
1 cup firmly packed brown sugar
2 eggs
1 teaspoon vanilla
1½ cups flour
1 teaspoon baking soda
½ teaspoon salt
3 cups quick or old-fashioned oats (not instant)
1 cup pecans, chopped •

1. Cover the raisins with hot water for 30 minutes to plump them. Drain and set aside.

2. Cream the butter with the sugars. Add the eggs and vanilla.

3. Stir the flour, baking soda and salt together. Add to the mixture. Stir in the oats, nuts and raisins.

4. Chill the dough at least 4 hours or overnight.

5. Preheat the oven to 375 degrees. Grease the baking sheets or line them with parchment paper.

6. Spoon about 2 tablespoons of dough for each cookie onto the baking sheets, allowing 2 inches between cookies.

7. Bake 8 to 10 minutes, switching the sheets on the shelves after 5 minutes. Bake until the cookies start to brown. Transfer them to racks to cool.

Note:
To freeze dough to bake another time, divide it into 3 or 4 skinny "sausages." Wrap each in plastic wrap. To bake, slice into rounds and bake as above.

• Taste nuts. If lacking flavor, toast them in a 300 degree oven on a dry cookie sheet for 20 minutes. Chop when cool.

Butter Almond Crisps

Makes about 48 cookies

These elegant Crisps are good with a cup of hot tea.

1 cup (2 sticks) butter
1 cup sugar minus 2 tablespoons
1 egg, separated
1 teaspoon vanilla
2 cups flour
¼ teaspoon cinnamon
½ cup slivered almonds

1. Preheat the oven to 300 degrees. Have ready 2 or more jelly-roll pans (rectangular baking pans with 1-inch-deep sides, usually 15½ x 10½-inches or 17 x 11-inches).

2. Cream the butter with the sugar. Stir in the egg yolk and the vanilla. Stir in the flour and the cinnamon.

3. With your hands, spread the batter in the jelly-roll pans as thinly as possible.

4. Brush with the egg white. Again, try to spread the dough even thinner. It may fill both pans plus an extra pan. Sprinkle with the almonds.

5. Bake 45 minutes, until the batter is firm and starts to brown. Immediately, cut the Crisps into squares and let them cool in the pan.

First Place: *TableTalk* Coffee Cake Contest

Adapted from *Carol Axelrod's Apple-Orange-Cinnamon Coffee Cake*.

Serves 12

This is a moist cake, loaded with flavor.

Streusel
1 cup packed dark brown sugar
1 cup peeled and diced apple
1 cup chopped walnuts
¼ cup flour
1 teaspoon cinnamon
3 tablespoons melted butter

Cake
½ cup (1 stick) butter
½ cup sugar
3 eggs
⅓ cup orange juice
½ teaspoon vanilla
2 cups flour
1 teaspoon baking soda
1 teaspoon baking powder
½ teaspoon salt
8 ounces sour cream

Glaze
½ cup powdered sugar
2-3 teaspoons orange juice

1. Preheat the oven to 350 degrees. Grease and flour a 9x13-inch pan. Mix the streusel ingredients; set aside.

2. On medium speed, cream the butter and sugar until light and fluffy. Add the eggs, one at a time, beating well after each addition. Add the orange juice and vanilla.

3. Stir the flour with the baking soda, baking powder and salt. On low speed, add the flour mixture to the batter alternately with the sour cream, in 5 parts beginning and ending with flour.

4. Spoon half the batter into the pan. Sprinkle with half the streusel. Spoon on remaining batter to make an even layer. Sprinkle on remaining streusel. Swirl batter with a knife to create a marble pattern. Bake 35 to 40 minutes, until a toothpick inserted in center comes out clean. Transfer to a rack to cool.

5. Blend the powdered sugar with the orange juice and spread it on the cake.

Patty Cake

Serves 12

This coffee cake is good for breakfast, brunch or supper. Don't use your mixer. It's best made by hand.

2¼ cups flour
½ teaspoon salt
2 teaspoons cinnamon, divided
¼ teaspoon ground ginger
1 cup packed brown sugar
¾ cup sugar
¾ cup corn oil
1 cup coarsely chopped pecans •
1 teaspoon baking soda
1 teaspoon baking powder
1 egg, beaten
1 cup buttermilk

1. Preheat the oven to 350 degrees. Grease a 9x13-inch pan. Combine the flour, salt, 1 teaspoon cinnamon, ginger, both sugars and oil. Stir only until the batter looks crumbly.

2. For the topping, remove ¾ cup of the batter. Combine it with the nuts and remaining cinnamon. Set it aside.

3. Stir the baking soda, baking powder, egg and buttermilk into the remaining batter. Mix lightly. Small lumps in batter are all right.

4. Pour the batter into the prepared pan. Spread the topping evenly over the cake. Bake 25-30 minutes or until a toothpick inserted in center comes out clean.

• Taste the nuts. If lacking flavor, toast them in a 300 degree oven on a dry cookie sheet for 20 minutes. Chop when cool.

Pear Cake

Serves 8

I clipped this from the *New York Times* years ago.

2 pounds ripe pears
Juice of 1 lemon, divided
½ cup (1 stick) plus 2 tablespoons butter at room temperature, divided
1 cup sugar, divided
2 eggs
1 cup flour
½ teaspoon baking powder
½ teaspoon salt
½ teaspoon almond extract
½ cup sliced almonds

1. Preheat the oven to 350 degrees. Grease and flour a 9-inch spring form cake pan.

2. Peel the pears. Cut them in half lengthwise. With a melon baller, remove cores and with paring knife, any remaining stems or cores. Place the pears cut side down on board and slice into ¼ inch wedges. Toss with half of the lemon juice. Set aside.

3. Cream ½ cup butter with ¾ cup sugar. Beat in the eggs, one at a time.

4. Stir the flour with baking powder and salt. Add to the batter, stirring lightly. Stir in the remaining lemon juice and almond extract.

5. Spread the batter in the prepared pan and cover evenly with sliced pears. (It is not necessary to arrange them artfully because they will almost disappear during baking.)

6. Scatter the almonds on top. Sprinkle with the remaining ¼ cup sugar, dot with the remaining 2 tablespoons butter. Bake 1 hour.

Sadie's Peanut Squares

Makes about 48 squares

My grandmother taught this traditional Belleville recipe to Mother when she moved there as a bride.

Cake
1 cup milk
1 tablespoon butter
1 teaspoon vanilla
4 eggs
2 cups sugar
¼ teaspoon salt
2 cups sifted flour
2 teaspoon baking powder

Frosting
½ cup (1 stick) butter, softened
1 pound powdered sugar (1 box)
1½ teaspoons vanilla
¾ cup milk, or enough to make a thin icing
1½ pounds salted Redskin Spanish peanuts with skins, finely ground but not to a
  paste

Cake
1. Preheat the oven to 325 degrees. Grease a 9 x 13-inch baking dish. Line it with waxed paper. Grease the paper and flour it, shaking out excess flour. Set aside.

2. Bring the milk and butter to boil in a saucepan. Remove from the heat and cool slightly. Stir in the vanilla. Set aside.

3. Beat the eggs with sugar and salt until thick and lemon colored. Stir the flour and baking powder together and fold into the eggs. Add the milk and stir until smooth.

4. Pour the batter into the prepared cake pan. Bake 20-30 minutes or until a cake tester comes out clean. Cool. Cake can be securely wrapped and frozen.

Frosting

1. Mix the butter with powdered sugar and vanilla.

2. Add the milk 1 tablespoon at a time to make a thin icing. You may not need all the milk, but you made need more later if the icing gets too thick.

3. Cut the cake into 48 squares, using a ruler and a sharp knife. 1¼ x 1¼-inches is good size. There will be some waste.

4. Ice each square on 5 sides. Roll in ground peanuts.

Don't Ask.
Don't Tell.

Maybe it's a mistake, but we always ask guests when we invite them to dinner if there is something they will not or cannot eat. Of course, we respect the wishes of those who can't eat certain foods or seasonings for medical reasons. But then, there are those who dislike the ordinary, for no apparent reason: "No potatoes, please; no sweet potatoes; no salmon; no beef, lamb or veal; no fish of any kind and, definitely, no cooked green vegetables." That puts the problem squarely in our laps, which I guess we deserve for asking in the first place.

Sometimes, people refrain from saying what they dislike. Our friend V. tells us he abhors fowl of any kind. I asked him what he does when served one or the other at someone's home. "I eat it," he said. "Maybe I do not eat it all, but I eat it." (His wife said he hides it under something else.)

That man deserves some kind of an award, unlike a gentleman who was my parents' dinner guest. Mother made superb apple pie, and he was well into his third piece when he asked, "Sadie, what makes this apple pie so good?" "Why, I use a lot of cinnamon," she said. With that, he put down his fork, leaving number three half finished. "I never eat cinnamon," he said.

It happened at our house when we served Sunshine Soup made of sweet potatoes, butternut squash, chicken broth and fresh ginger. It is light, good tasting and remarkably healthy. "Yum," our guest said. "What is it?" That was my mistake. Billy has asked me not to give recipes at the table. I told her, and, as did the apple pie eater, she put down her spoon. "I don't like sweet potatoes," she said.

What causes violent dislikes for seemingly common mild foods? I consulted my yellowing copy of *Consuming Passions, the Anthology of Eating* by George Armelagos and Peter Farb, long out of print but one of the most valuable books of its kind. I read that early impressions of childhood have strong influences on preferences in adult life. Maybe V. witnessed a chicken being killed. Maybe our friend's mother made her sit at the table until she ate her sweet potatoes. Perhaps my mother's guest took cough medicine flavored with cinnamon. Associations evidently linger into adulthood.

So, back to the dinner guests whom one wishes to please, what does one do? Send each guest a list of foods to be checked off and returned to sender? Create a database for your friends to keep life simple? Refuse to invite Joe and Joan together because he eats fish and she won't?

Or maybe we should simply follow the rule, "Don't ask. Don't tell."

Sadie's Apple Crisp

Serves 8

This is Mother's apple pie turned upside down, since piecrusts have gone out of fashion in our house. She believed in lots of cinnamon and long slow baking.

8 cups peeled, cored and sliced apples, about 3 pounds
1½ cups sugar, divided
1 tablespoon ground cinnamon
½ teaspoon nutmeg
1½ cups flour
½ teaspoon salt
½ cup (1 stick) chilled butter

1. Preheat the oven to 350 degrees. Grease a 2-quart baking dish or 8 individual baking dishes.

2. Toss the apples with 1 cup of the sugar, the cinnamon and the nutmeg. Spread them in the baking dish.

3. Put the flour, the salt and the remaining sugar in the bowl of a food processor. Pulse briefly. Cut the chilled butter in 16 pieces and add it to the food processor. Pulse only until the mixture is combined and looks like coarse corn meal. Spread the topping evenly over the apples.

4. Bake about 1½ hours or until the apples are tender and the topping is golden brown. Serve with ice cream or whipped cream.

Note:
If prepared hours before serving, the Crisp can be reheated in a warm oven or in a microwave.

First Place: *TableTalk* Strudel Contest

Adapted from *Rita Michelson's Strudel*.

Makes about 60 slices

No more fear of strudel with this prize-winning recipe.

3 cups apricot preserves
1 cup dried apricots, chopped
2 cups flour
1 teaspoon sugar
⅛ teaspoon salt
⅓ cup water
¼ cup vegetable oil
1 egg, lightly beaten
1 cup sugar
2 teaspoons cinnamon
¾ cup (1½ sticks) melted butter, divided
1½ cups golden raisins, divided
2 cups chopped pecans, • divided
Powdered sugar to garnish

1. The day before or several hours before baking strudel, combine the apricot preserves with dried apricots. Set aside.

2. Preheat the oven to 350 degrees. Spray cookie sheets with non-stick cooking spray. To prepare the dough, combine the flour, 1 teaspoon sugar and the salt in a large mixing bowl.

3. Bring the water and oil to a boil; stir into the dry ingredients. The mixture will be crumbly. When cool, stir in the egg. Cover and set it aside for 15 minutes.

4. Divide the dough into 4 portions. Roll one portion at a time into an oblong sheet. Keep the rest of the dough covered.

5. Combine the sugar and cinnamon. Set 2 tablespoons of it aside for the tops.

6. Spread 3 tablespoons of melted butter over the dough. Sprinkle it with a scant fourth cup of the sugar/cinnamon mixture, 3 tablespoons raisins and 4 tablespoons pecans.

7. Arrange one quarter of the apricot mixture at bottom of the wide end of the sheet and roll it from bottom to top. Place the strudel on the cookie sheet, seam side down. Score into 15 (3/4–inch) slices and sprinkle with 2 teaspoons of the sugar/cinnamon.

8. Continue with remaining dough and filling. Bake the strudel 25-30 minutes.

9. Carefully, lift the hot strudel onto racks. Slice through where scored. Sprinkle with powdered sugar.

• Taste pecans. If lacking flavor, toast them in a 300 degree oven on a dry cookie sheet for 20 minutes. Chop when cool.

Lemon Pistachio Squares or Tart

Makes 16 bars or 8 tart servings

Crust
¼ cup shelled pistachios
1 cup flour
½ cup powdered sugar
¼ teaspoon kosher salt
½ cup (1 stick) cold unsalted butter, cut into small chunks

Filling
¼ cup shelled pistachios
2 eggs
1 cup sugar
½ teaspoon baking powder
2 tablespoons flour
1 teaspoon grated lemon zest (yellow outermost layer of peel)
¼ cup fresh lemon juice
Powdered sugar to garnish

Crust
1. Preheat the oven to 350 degrees.

2. Coarsely chop the pistachios in a food processor.

3. Add the flour, sugar and salt to the food processor and pulse a few times.

4. Add the butter and pulse only until the mixture looks crumbly. Press the crumbs into the bottom and sides of a 9 x 9-inch pan or a 9-inch tart pan. Bake until lightly browned, about 18-20 minutes.

Filling
1. Coarsely chop the pistachios in a food processor.

2. Add the eggs, sugar, baking powder, flour, grated lemon zest and lemon juice. Pulse a few seconds and set aside.

3. When the crust is ready, pulse the filling a few seconds. Pour it into the crust and bake about 20-25 minutes until it is set in center and a toothpick inserted in the center comes out clean. Let it cool on a rack.

4. Cut into 2-inch squares or into 8 tart slices. Sift powdered sugar on top after cutting. (It hides cracks, should there be any.)

Lemon Pecan Bars

Makes 4 dozen bars

Lemon Pecan Bars were one of my first baking endeavors in 1950.

Crust
¼ cup sugar
1¼ cups flour
¼ teaspoon salt
1 egg
½ teaspoon vanilla
½ cup (1 stick) cold butter

Filling
2 eggs
1½ cups packed brown sugar
½ cup grated sweetened coconut
2 tablespoons flour
½ teaspoon baking powder
½ teaspoon salt
1 cup chopped pecans •
1 teaspoon vanilla

Frosting
1½ cups powdered sugar
Lemon zest (grated yellow outermost layer of peel)
Juice of 1 lemon

1. Preheat oven to 350 degrees. In food processor, combine the sugar, flour and salt. Pulse a few times. Add the egg and vanilla and pulse a few seconds.

2. Cut the cold butter into small pieces. Add it to the bowl and pulse a few seconds, until the dough looks like coarse corn meal.

3. Spread and pat the dough in a 9 x 13-inch pan. Bake 15 minutes or until it looks firm and is beginning to brown.

4. Combine all the filling ingredients and gently spread the filling over the hot crust. Bake 25 minutes.

5. Combine the powdered sugar with lemon zest and enough lemon juice to form a thick icing. While hot, gently frost the top. Cut into bars when cool.

• Taste pecans. If lacking flavor, toast them in 300-degree oven on a dry cookie sheet for 20 minutes. Chop when cool.

Peaches and Cream Tart

Serves 10-12

Make it only with good summer peaches.

2 cups flour
½ teaspoon salt
1 cup sugar or more depending on sweetness of peaches, divided
½ cup (1 stick) cold butter, cut into small pieces
8-10 unpeeled peaches, halved and seeded
2 teaspoons cinnamon
4 egg yolks, slightly beaten
2 cups sour cream

1. Preheat the oven to 400 degrees. Grease a (10½-inch) tart pan.

2. Combine the flour, salt and ¼ cup sugar in a food processor. Pulse 5 seconds.

3. Add the cold butter and pulse about 10 seconds until the mixture looks like coarse cornmeal. Pour the crumbs into the prepared pan. Using hands and fingers, press the crumbs evenly onto the sides and bottom of the pan.

4. Slice 1 or 2 of the peaches. Arrange the remaining halves over the crust, cut side down. Fill in the gaps with peach slices. Mix the cinnamon with the remaining sugar and sprinkle over the peaches. Add the extra sugar if the peaches are not sweet enough. Bake 15 minutes.

5. Combine the egg yolks with sour cream. Spread over the top of the tart. Bake 30 minutes more. Serve warm or cold.

Berry Buckle

Serves 8

This recipe is from Chef Bill Cardwell of Cardwell's at the Plaza. His mother made it for him when he was a child back in Vermont.

8 cups any kind of berries or peaches or a combination
1 to 2 tablespoons sugar, optional
2 teaspoons grated lemon zest (yellow outermost layer of the peel)
1 cup flour
1 cup sugar
1 teaspoon baking powder
1 egg
½ cup (1 stick) butter, melted

1. Preheat the oven to 350 degrees. Toss the fruit with sugar if it is tart.

2. Place the fruit in even layer in an 8 x 8-inch pan. Top with lemon zest. Or fill 8 individual baking dishes with 1 cup fruit and top each with ¼ teaspoon lemon zest.

3. With a fork, stir the flour, sugar, baking powder and egg into a crumbly mixture. Sprinkle evenly over the fruit. For individual dishes, spread about ¼ cup on each baking dish.

4. Pour melted butter over crumbs. For individual dishes, pour about 1 tablespoon over each.

5. Bake the Buckle until bubbly and golden brown, about 30 to 40 minutes. Serve warm with ice cream or whipped cream.

6. The Buckle can be made early in the day and reheated in a warm oven or microwave just before serving.

Blackberry Cobbler

Serves 8-10

I came across this recipe when researching southern cooking. After baking, the berries are on the bottom of the cobbler with the crust on top.

Batter
1 cup flour
1 tablespoon baking powder
1 cup sugar
¼ teaspoon salt
1 cup evaporated milk
1 teaspoon vanilla

Blackberry Filling
3 cups blackberries, fresh or frozen
1 tablespoon cornstarch
½ cup boiling water
¾ cup sugar
2 tablespoons butter
1 teaspoon cinnamon

1. Preheat the oven to 350 degrees. Grease a 9 x 12-inch pan.

2. Combine the batter ingredients and pour them into the prepared pan.

3. Combine the berries, cornstarch, water and sugar. Pour slowly into the middle of the cobbler batter. Dot with the butter and sprinkle with cinnamon. Bake 45-55 minutes or until the cobbler is firm and lightly browned.

The Language Barrier

The late Alistair Cooke, British host of *Masterpiece Theatre*, often quoted George Bernard Shaw's dictum that the United States and Great Britain are two nations divided by a common language.

How true we found those words to be when our English friends, John and Mary Foster, came to visit. On their first morning, as we were about to go sightseeing, Mary asked us to wait while she put on her jumper. I thought she was changing her skirt and blouse for a sleeveless dress worn with a blouse. But her jumper was a sweater, which went into the trunk (the boot, she called it), as the day got warmer.

Over the course of the week, we went the Opera Theatre, Zoo, Art Museum, Pulitzer Foundation, Missouri History Museum and the Missouri Botanical Garden, where it drizzled, making them feel at home. By four in the afternoon, after a day of sightseeing, I was ready for a nap, but the Fosters wanted hot tea, even though it was 85 degrees with high humidity. Here was another barrier—not of language but of style. I made them tea my way: a tea bag plopped into a cup filled with hot water from our hot water dispenser. The Fosters were too polite to say that I should have brought fresh tap water just to a boil and allowed the tea to steep in it for several minutes. They drank their tea with a plate of biscuits (cookies) and "a dash of milk, please."

The *American Heritage Dictionary* calls a dash a small amount of an added ingredient. My *Oxford Quick Reference Dictionary*, purchased a few years ago in England, calls it a "slight admixture, especially of a liquid."

To span the language barrier in culinary matters, the Fosters bought us *Delia Smith's Complete Cookery Course*. Smith is England's most popular cookbook writer, but I think that in America, she would surely need a translator: chips are french fries; "grilling" in England is broiling; "offal" refers to kidneys, liver, tongue, oxtails, tripe and heart, which have their own section in her book; porridge is our oatmeal; pulses are beans and dried peas; swedes are rutabagas; pudding is a generic for dessert and a custard is a mixture thin enough to pour over the pudding.

In addition to offal and the usual cookbook sections, Smith has a chapter on leftovers. She writes, "However well we plan, and however meticulous we are, we all have food left over at times and it would be criminal not to put it to good use."

Apple Raisin Bread Pudding

Makes 6 servings

When you're long on bread, turn it into Apple Raisin Bread Pudding.

1 cup hot milk
2 cups coarse fresh bread crumbs from dense bread, crusts removed
2 eggs
½ cup firmly packed brown sugar
1 teaspoon cinnamon
½ teaspoon salt
½ teaspoon vanilla
½ teaspoon grated lemon zest (yellow outer layer of the lemon)
½ cup raisins
1 apple, peeled and thinly sliced
2 tablespoons butter

1. Preheat the oven to 350 degrees. Grease a 1-quart baking dish.

2. Pour the hot milk over the crumbs and set aside about 20 minutes for the bread to absorb some of the milk.

3. Lightly beat the eggs with the sugar, cinnamon, salt, vanilla and lemon zest. When the bread and milk have cooled, stir in the eggs.

4. Stir in the raisins and the apple. Pour into the baking dish. Dot with the butter.

5. Place the pudding dish in a larger baking pan in the oven. Pour hot water halfway up the sides of the pudding dish. Bake about 1 hour, until a knife inserted in the center comes out clean and the pudding is beginning to brown.

Grand Slam Cheese Pie

Serve 16

I have no idea where this dessert got its name, but it's been around a long time. This recipe might be older than I am. It was one of Mother's favorites.

1 (12-ounce) can evaporated milk
½ cup (1 stick) butter
1 (3-ounce) package lemon gelatin
1 cup boiling water
½ cup (1 stick) butter, melted
2 cups graham cracker crumbs, purchased or rolled from 16 double crackers
1 tablespoon sugar
1 tablespoon flour
½ teaspoon cinnamon
1 (8-ounce) package low-fat cream cheese
1 cup sugar
1 teaspoon vanilla
1 lemon, its juice and zest

1. Put the can of evaporated milk in the freezer for 1 hour. Then refrigerate it until you are ready to whip it. Refrigerate the mixing bowl and beaters.

2. Dissolve the lemon gelatin in the boiling water. Set it aside to cool and thicken.

3. For the crust, melt the butter in a saucepan. Mix the crumbs, sugar, flour and cinnamon into the butter. Set aside ⅓ cup crumbs for the top of the cakes. Press the crumbs into 2 (9-inch) pie pans or a 9 x 13-inch pan.

4. Whip the evaporated milk until firm peaks form. Set it aside.

5. Mix the cream cheese with the sugar, vanilla, lemon juice, zest and the thickened gelatin. Fold the mixture into the whipped evaporated milk. Pour into the prepared pans. Refrigerate or freeze.

Tuiles

Serves 12

Frank Waldman, a former St.Louis chef, taught me to make Tuiles. Originally, these cookies were molded while hot over a rolling pin, making them look like the tile (or tuile) of roofs. I prefer them shaped like a small bowl to be filled with fruit or ice cream.

Oil to grease cookie sheet
2 eggs
2 egg whites
1 cup granulated sugar
1 cup sliced almonds •
¼ cup flour ••
½ teaspoon almond extract

1. Preheat the oven to 400 degrees. Grease a heavy non-stick cookie sheet. Grease 2 (12-ounce) custard cups on the inside or outside, depending on how you wish to shape the tuile.

2. Combine all the ingredients.

3. Bake only 2 tuiles on a sheet. Drop about 1½ tablespoons of batter for each tuile on each end of the cookie sheet. With the back of spoon, spread the batter into 6-inch circle. It is all right if there are some holes in the dough or if the tuile is not round. These are free-form cookies.

4. Bake the tulles about 5 to 7 minutes or until light brown. They will not color evenly. Immediately, remove them from sheet with a spatula and while they are hot, mold them in or over the greased custard cup. If you mangle a tuile, return it to oven for a few minutes and try again.

5. Tuiles will crisp and cool almost immediately and can be lifted off the mold. Continue with the remaining batter.

6. To freeze them, stack them in an oversize container so they will not break. You can also freeze them flat, layering them with waxed paper. To serve, put them on a cookie sheet in a 400 degree oven for a few minutes and then shape as above. If the weather is warm or damp, keep them frozen.

- Instead of almonds and almond extract, try 1 cup chopped hazelnuts with 1 teaspoon dark rum or 1 cup chopped walnuts with 1 teaspoon cognac or 1 cup chopped pecans with 1 teaspoon Jack Daniels.

•• For Passover, replace the flour with 1 tablespoon matzo cake meal and 3 tablespoons potato starch.

Index